Dear Nick,

Sorry to miss
you at Sarah's
wonderful lunch.

Best wishes

James

SPORT'S GREAT ALL-ROUNDERS

A BIOGRAPHICAL DICTIONARY

JAMES HOLDER

authorHOUSE®

AuthorHouse™ UK
1663 Liberty Drive
Bloomington, IN 47403 USA
www.authorhouse.co.uk
Phone: 0800.197.4150

Published by AuthorHouse 08/25/2015

ISBN: 978-1-5049-4585-1 (sc)
ISBN: 978-1-5049-4586-8 (hc)
ISBN: 978-1-5049-4569-1 (e)

Contents

Ackowledgements

Since I first came up with the idea of writing this book, a number of people have provided guidance and encouragement in some form or other; they know who they are but I would like to acknowledge and thank the following in particular: Anthony Forbes-Watson, Mike Doggart, Ross Curzon-Butler and Andy Byrd at Bravo6, Nick Walford and Chris Lane. In addition I would like to thank my parents for the encouragement they gave myself and my siblings to play and enjoy sport. And lastly, my final thanks go to the best all-rounder of them all, my wife Annabel, for her support and patience.

Introduction

On a number of occasions over recent years, the performance of a sportsperson has led a number of commentators to claim that the performance in question has made the sportsperson in question the greatest of all time. At different times, it has been the turn of Roger Federer to be mooted as the greatest tennis player of all time, Tiger Woods the greatest golfer of all time and Usain Bolt the greatest athlete of all time; and recently, Floyd Mayweather has even claimed that he might be the greatest boxer of all time. These claims may well be valid but less frequently is the greatness of all-round sportspersons commented upon.

It should come as no surprise that there are a large number of talented sportsmen and sportswomen who have excelled not just in the sport for which they are best known. The likes of Nigel Mansell, Tim Henman, Don Bradman, Gary Sobers, Ted Dexter and Alan Hansen are all, or were in their prime, very competent golfers but they are all better known for their achievements in other sports. Indeed it would be surprising if someone with a good eye for a ball was only competent in one ball sport although, in his book Playing The Moldovans At Tennis, Tony Hawks proved that not all sportsmen are necessarily good at other sports, when he won his bet that he, a good club player, could beat at tennis all of the then current Moldovan football team.

Before sport became as professional as it is now and when certain sports, such as football, rugby and cricket, tended to be more seasonal, it was easier for sportsmen and, to a lesser extent, sportswomen to play more than one sport to a very high standard; but, with so many sports now being played all-year round, it is less easy for those who are talented in more than one sport to show their talent beyond one sport. Brian Clough's first job as manager of Derby County was to transfer Ian Buxton because he also played cricket for Derbyshire and was therefore not available at the beginning of the football season, something Clough was not willing to accept. More recently, the Australian Ellyse Perry has committed herself to cricket which has resulted in her not being selected for the national football team.

Not since 1958, when Arthur Milton became the 12th man to do so, has a man played football and cricket for England. Coincidentally, not since the same year, when Milton's opening partner M. J. K. Smith became the seventh man to do so, has a man played both cricket and rugby for England. Of the 19 sportsmen who have played either cricket and football for England or cricket and rugby for England, eight did so in the 19th century, when there were less professional sportsmen and the opportunities for gifted sportsmen to play more than one sport at the top level were greater; and the three who have played both football and rugby for England all did so in the 19th century.

For others though, professionalism has made it easier for them to excel in more than one sport; for example, when rugby union dropped its amateur status, a number of rugby league players switched codes and became internationals in both rugby union and rugby league; even though some rugby players have not coped with the switch as well as others, to date more than 200 rugby players have represented their countries at both rugby union and rugby league; the similarity between the two codes of rugby would suggest though not so much evidence of multi-talent, but more so of talent at rugby generally.

A number of very well-known sportsmen are also well known for playing more than one sport. For example, Ian Botham turned out for Scunthorpe United at football, something which received more publicity than is usually accorded to Scunthorpe United footballers, no doubt as much because of his personality and cricketing achievements as for his footballing skills. It is less well known that another England cricket captain, Brian Close, also played professional football, for Bradford City; and Botham's great friend Viv Richards, one of the greatest batsmen of all time, arguably went one better than both of them in turning out for his country Antigua at football, making him the only man to have played in both the football and cricket World Cups, albeit, in the case of football, only in the qualifying rounds.

In looking at who are the greatest all-rounders, account should also to be taken of the different skills required in performing well in different sports. To illustrate, of the 80+ Olympians who have medals in more than one sport, a number have done so because the sports in question require similar skills. Johnny Weissmuller, later to become Tarzan, not only won Olympic golds at swimming, but also won a bronze at water polo, where no doubt his ability at swimming was a great asset. Only one person, the American Frank Kugler, has won Olympic medals in three different sports; at the 1904 Olympics, Kugler won bronze medals for wrestling, weightlifting and the tug-of-war but his success though is unquestionably down to his strength and the ability to use it in more than one sport. Four years earlier, three Frenchmen had the distinction of winning the same medals in two different sports, when each of them won a gold medal as members of the rugby team which won gold and of the tug-of-war team which won silver; it is easy to assume that the skills they learned playing rugby provided them with the necessary qualities to perform successfully in the tug-of-war.

In this book are listed, in alphabetical order, the 172 sportsmen and sportswomen I have selected who have excelled at more than one sport. Of the 172, 63 are English, eight Scottish, three Welsh and three Irish; 26 are New Zealanders, 18 South Africans and 14 Australians; the others come from the USA (nine), Germany (four), Canada, India and Norway (three each), Italy, Russia, Switzerland, the West Indies and Zimbabwe (two each) and Austria, Kenya, Namibia, Singapore and Spain (one each). Of the 172, 26 are women and nine are disabled. 105 of the 146 men listed have represented their country in more than one sport and of these 105, 31 did so before the outbreak of World War I in 1914 and only 28 have done so since 1960; in the case of the 26 women listed, 24 have represented their country in more than one sport, but, in contrast to the men, only three did so before 1960.

The 172 sportsmen and sportswomen listed played 39 different sports, with cricket the most popular – 118 of those listed were or are cricketers;

after cricket, in descending order, come rugby (60), football (58), hockey (25), tennis (17), athletics (15), cycling and golf (12 each), skiing (11), swimming (six), baseball, boxing and ice hockey (five each), American football, basketball, speed skating and squash (four each), badminton (three), Aussie rules football, bobsleigh, fencing, lacrosse, motor racing, rugby league, table tennis and water polo (two each) and angling, archery, billiards, bowls, canoeing, handball, mountaineering, rowing, sailing, shooting, snooker, surfing and wrestling (one each).

It is by no means an exhaustive list and there are many more who have performed at the top level in more than one sport. Included though are the three men who have played both rugby and football for England, the 12 men who have played both football and cricket for England and the seven men who have played both rugby and cricket for England; but of the 21 other Englishmen who have played cricket for England and professional football, only nine are included – the other 12 are listed in Appendix 1; of the 68 others who have played football for England and first-class cricket, only six are included – the other 62 are listed in Appendix 2; there are another 56 who played first-class cricket and professional football for an English club, but only three are included. Similarly with rugby players, there are 79 men who have represented their country at both rugby and cricket and a further 15 who have represented one country at rugby and another country at cricket; of these 94 dual rugby and cricket internationals, only 36 are included – in the case of those not included, either the country they played for at cricket is not a Test-playing country or the country they played for at rugby is not one of the six leading European rugby nations who play in the Six Nations or one of the four leading Southern Hemisphere nations who play in the Rugby Championships, but their names are listed in Appendix 3. A further 169 have played rugby for their country and first-class cricket but only six of them are included, as the rest, although clearly good at more than one sport, only represented their country in one sport. Some of those included did not have distinguished careers in the sports for which they represented their country, but they did at least have the distinction of representing their country in more than one sport.

I have not included triathletes such as Jonathan and Alistair Brownlee who, to have been as successful as they have been in their sport, have needed to be accomplished sportsmen in three sports, but only compete in triathlons and not separately in the three sports. For the same reason, I have not included pentathletes, heptathletes or decathletes. The list is therefore made up mostly, although not entirely, of those who have represented their country in more than one sport or who have played more than two sports for top flight clubs; I have included a few though who performed at the highest level in one sport or in World Cup finals but also played another sport to a very high or professional standard.

Finally, readers are invited to submit the names of any other sportsmen and sportswomen who they feel are worthy of inclusion in this book, by forwarding the names of such sportsmen and sportswomen, with brief details of their sporting achievements, to james@thesportsgreatest.com. Readers are also invited to submit to the same email address the names of those who, in their view, are (i) the world's greatest all-round sportsman, (ii) the world's greatest all-round sportswoman, (iii) the UK's greatest all-round sportsman and (iv) the UK's greatest all-round sportswoman.

1.   Les Ames (1905-1990), *English cricketer and footballer*

Les Ames was born in Elham, Kent in 1905.

Ames played cricket for Kent from 1926 until 1951, during which time he broke a number of wicketkeeping and batting records. In his 593 first-class games, he scored a total of 37,248 runs, averaging 43.51; having scored 102 centuries, with a top score of 295, he remains the only wicketkeeper to have scored a century of centuries. As a wicketkeeper, he took a total of 703 catches and made 418 stumpings, the highest number of stumpings in first-class cricket – 259 of these stumpings were made standing up to the leg-breaks and googlies of Tich Freeman. His occasional bowling also brought him 24 wickets at an average of 33.37.

Ames played in 47 Test matches for England, including in the infamous Bodyline series in 1932/33. In Tests, he scored 2,434 runs, including eight centuries and a top score of 147, at an average of 43.51 and took 74 catches and made 23 stumpings.

In 1931, Ames played football for Gillingham in five of their matches and scored one goal for them.

During the Second World War, Ames served with the RAF, rising to the rank of Squadron-Leader; after retiring from playing cricket, Ames became a selector and managed MCC overseas tours, before becoming secretary and manager of Kent County Cricket Club.

Ames died in 1990 at the age of 84; in his obituary in Wisden 1991, he was described as the greatest wicketkeeper-batsman of all time, and, in his book The Top 100 Cricketers Of All Time, Christopher Martin-Jenkins only listed Adam Gilchrist and Kumar Sangakkara ahead of Ames as wicketkeeper/batsmen.

2. Biddy Anderson (1874-1926), *South African cricketer and rugby player*

James Henry "Biddy" Anderson is one of six South Africans to have represented his country at both cricket and rugby.

Anderson was born in Kimberley in 1874. He was selected to play at centre for the national rugby team in 1896 against the touring Great Britain team. He played in all three matches against Great Britain, winning the final one but losing the first two; in the final Test, Anderson's pass to Alf Lerard led to Lerard scoring under the posts for the first score of the match and to South Africa recording their first Test match win at rugby.

Anderson also played cricket for Western Provence and, in 1902, was picked to play against Australia in the first Test series between the two countries; he was a right-hand batsman and was picked as captain in place of Henry Taberer in the second Test, which was won by Australia; he only played in the one Test, in which he scored 32 and 11 and took one catch. His first-class cricket career consisted of 14 matches in which he scored a total of 511 runs, including a top score of 109, at an average of 23.22; he also bowled four overs in first-class cricket taking one wicket for 26 runs.

Later in life he became a racehorse breeder; he died in 1926 at the age of 51. In his obituary in the Cape Times of 11th March 1926, Percy Twentyman-Jones (see Chapter 153) wrote that "so long as rugby football is discussed in South Africa, the name of Biddy Anderson as the prince of South African three-quarters will keep cropping up".

3. Rob Andrew (1963-   ), *English rugby player and cricketer*

Rob Andrew was born in Richmond, Yorkshire in 1963.

During a rugby-playing career which started in 1982 and ended in 1999, Andrew was a fly-half who played first for Cambridge University, then Nottingham, then Wasps and finally Newcastle Falcons. He was first picked to play for England in 1985 and, over the next 13 years, played 71 times for them, 50 of which were won by England. As well as taking part in the Rugby World Cups in 1987, 1991 (when England reached the final but lost to Australia 12-6) and 1995, he played in the England team which won the Grand Slam in 1991, 1992 and 1995. His points tally for England was 396 points, made up of two tries, 33 conversions, 86 penalties and 21 drop goals, including one in the last minute to win their World Cup match against Australia in 1995, a feat repeated by Jonny Wilkinson when England won the Rugby World Cup in 2003.

Andrew was also picked for the British and Irish Lions tours to Australia in 1989 and to New Zealand in 1993; on the Australian tour, which the Lions won 2-1, Andrew played in the two games won by the Lions and, on the New Zealand tour which New Zealand won 2-1, he played in all three matches. His points tally for the Lions was 11 points (one conversion, one penalty and two drop goals).

Andrew also played first-class cricket, playing in 17 games for Cambridge University in 1984 and 1985. In these matches, he scored 658 runs at an average of 21.22, with a top score of 101 not out; he also took 12 wickets at an average of 70.58. He also played cricket for Yorkshire 2nd XI and whilst bowling for them, he took the wicket of the future England captain, Mike Atherton, for a duck.

Andrew retired from international rugby in 1995, the year he was awarded the MBE for services to rugby; since retiring from playing rugby, Andrew has continued to be heavily involved in the game, first as director at Newcastle and more recently as England's director of elite rugby at the RFU. He is also President of the rugby charity, Wooden Spoon.

4. Johnny Arnold (1907-1984), *English cricketer and footballer*

Johnny Arnold is one of 12 Englishmen to have played both football and cricket for England.

Arnold was born in Cowley, Oxford in 1907.

His football career began with Oxford City and, in July 1928, he was signed by Southampton F C. He made 110 appearances at outside-left for Southampton, in which he scored 46 goals, before moving in February 1933 to Fulham; he played 213 games and scored 62 goals for Fulham before retiring in 1939. In 1933, he was selected to play for England against Scotland in the Home Internationals, a match which England lost 1-2; he was not selected to play for England again.

Arnold's cricket career started with Oxfordshire for whom he played in the Minor Counties league. By moving to Southampton where he was playing his football, Arnold qualified to play cricket for Hampshire, for whom he played from 1929 until 1950. In his second year playing cricket for Hampshire, following the retirement of Jack Hobbs and the absence through injury of Herbert Sutcliffe, he was selected to open the batting for England in their Test against New Zealand. In his two innings, he scored 0 and 34 and was not selected again to play for England.

By the time of his retirement in 1950, Arnold had played a total of 402 first-class matches, scoring a total of 21,831 runs, including a top score of 227 and a total of 37 hundreds, at an average of 32.82; his occasional bowling brought him 17 wickets at an average of 69.52.

After his retirement as a cricketer, Arnold ended up as an umpire, a role he carried out from 1960 until 1974.

Arnold died in 1984, aged 76.

5. Claude Ashton (1901-1942), *English footballer, cricketer and hockey player*

Claude Ashton was born in Calcutta in 1901.

After leaving Winchester College, where he was captain of cricket, football, rackets and fives, Ashton went up to Cambridge University where he won his blue in football, hockey and cricket.

In the 1921 cricket Varsity match against Oxford, he played alongside his brothers Gilbert, who was the Cambridge captain and Hubert; Hubert and Claude also played in the Varsity match a year later when Hubert was captain. Claude emulated his brothers by captaining the Cambridge team in 1923, but without his brothers' success, Cambridge losing the 1923 match by an innings, after having won both the 1921 and 1922 matches by an innings.

After leaving university, Ashton continued playing for Essex and, by the time he retired in 1938, had, over a career spanning 18 years, played 127 games of first-class cricket, scoring 4,723 runs at an average of 24.98 with four centuries and a top score of 118 and taking 139 wickets at an average of 30.92, with best figures of seven for 52.

Ashton also kept up his football after graduating and played for the leading amateur club Corinthian; his success with Corinthian, for whom he scored 145 goals in 208 games, brought him national recognition and, as well as appearing in 12 amateur internationals for England, also made one appearance for the full national side, captaining them in his one full international, a goalless draw against Northern Ireland in 1925.

After hanging up his football boots, Ashton took up hockey again, joining the Beckenham club and earning himself an England trial.

Ashton qualified as a chartered accountant before working at the London Stock Exchange; he died in 1942 at the age of 41 following a mid-air collision whilst out flying on a training exercise during the Second World War.

6. Benjamin Howard Baker (1892-1987), *English Olympic athlete, footballer and cricketer*

Benjamin Howard Baker was born in Liverpool in 1892.

Baker represented Great Britain at the Olympics in 1912 and 1920. At the 1912 Olympics, he took part in the high jump, coming 11th and in the standing high jump competition, coming 16th; eight years later he took part in the high jump and triple jump, coming sixth in the high jump and 8th in the triple jump. He was AAA champion at the high jump six times and, in 1921, broke the British high jump record with a jump of 6 feet 5 inches, a record which stood for 26 years. In addition to jumping, he was also accomplished at the hurdles, discus, hammer and javelin.

In addition to his talents as an athlete, Baker also played football. Throughout his football career, he retained his status as an amateur but this did not stop him representing the full England side, including professionals, on two occasions. As well as playing in goal for England in eight amateur internationals, he also played for the full team against Belgium in 1921 (which England won 2-0) and against Northern Ireland in 1925 (which was drawn 0-0). He played 13 times for Everton, twice in 1921 and 11 times between 1926 and 1928 and once for Oldham Athletic in the 1928/29 season but most of his football was spent playing for Chelsea, for whom he played 93 games, between 1921 and 1926.

As well as being an athlete and a footballer, Baker played cricket for Liverpool Cricket Club and the Lancashire 2nd XI and was close to being selected at water polo for England. In the Liverpool Harriers website, it is stated that he also played tennis at Wimbledon and, although he became an honorary councillor of the Lawn Tennis Association, there is no record of him taking part in the Men's Singles at the Wimbledon Championships.

Baker died in 1987, at the age of 95.

7. Snowy Baker (1884-1953), *Australian swimmer, boxer and rugby player*

Reginald Leslie Baker, better known as Snowy Baker, was born in Sydney in 1884.

By the age of 13, he was the New South Wales swimming champion over the distances of 110 yards and 220 yards and at the age of 17, the New South Wales middleweight boxing champion; a year later, he was crowned the Australian middleweight and heavyweight champion.

Baker also played rugby for New South Wales and, in 1904, was selected to play scrum-half for Australia in two Tests against the touring Great Britain team, matches which Great Britain won 17-0 and 17-3.

In 1908, Baker competed at the London Olympics in the swimming, diving and boxing events; his only medal came in the middleweight boxing event, in which he won the silver medal, losing to Great Britain's Johnny Douglas (see Chapter 40) in the final; like Baker, Douglas represented his country in more than one sport, captaining England at cricket and playing football for the England amateur team.

Baker also excelled in a number of other sports, including water polo, rowing, running and cricket and was an accomplished rider, as well as being more than competent at surfing, fencing, hockey and sailing.

Following a motor car accident, Baker tried his hand at boxing promotion, before becoming a silent movie star and finally settling in America.

In his biography, The Snowy Baker Story by Greg Growden, it is claimed Baker excelled in no less than 26 different sports and, in addition to representing Australia at swimming, diving and boxing at the Olympics and at rugby, he also represented them as a horseman, whilst other reports suggest he also represented Australia at water polo; in the same book, it is claimed that, during his time in Hollywood, he taught Rudolph Valentino to kiss and Elizabeth Taylor to ride for the film National Velvet and played polo with Walt Disney and Clark Gable.

Baker died at the age of 69 from cerebrovascular disease.

8. Chris Balderstone (1940-2000), *English cricketer and footballer*

Chris Balderstone was born in Huddersfield in 1940.

Balderstone was a midfield player whose football career started as a youth with Shrewsbury Town before Bill Shankly signed him to join Huddersfield Town in May 1958, promising to make him the finest wing-half in the world. Between then and June 1965, when he left to join Carlisle United, he played 117 games for Huddersfield, scoring 24 goals for them. He stayed at Carlisle until 1976 during which time he played 376 league games for them and scored 68 goals; his penalty against Tottenham Hotspur in Carlisle's third game of the 1974/75 season took them to the top of Division 1, then the top division of English league football. Carlisle's early form that season was not maintained and, by the end of the season, they were relegated.

Balderstone moved from Carlisle to Doncaster Rovers in 1976 where he only played for one season before finishing his career at Queen of the South, for whom he played 34 games over two seasons. He played a total of 39 games for Doncaster, scoring only once. His game for Doncaster against Brentford on 15th September 1976 was an evening game; earlier in the day, Balderstone had scored 51 not out for Leicestershire against Derbyshire, making him the first player to turn out for a league football match and a county cricket match on the same day; he returned the following day to complete his century and take three Derbyshire wickets.

Whilst he was at Carlisle, Balderstone was spending the summers playing cricket as a right-hand batsman and left-arm slow orthodox bowler, first for Yorkshire and then Leicestershire. He played his first game for Yorkshire in 1961 and, before following in the footsteps of former England captain, Ray Illingworth and joining Leicestershire in 1971, he played a total of 67 first-class matches for Yorkshire.

In 1976, Balderstone was picked to play in the final two Test matches against the touring West Indies; in his two matches, he only managed 39 runs at an average of 9.75 and took one wicket for 96 runs against a West Indian team boasting a very strong batting and bowling line-up. After being bowled twice for a duck by Michael Holding in his second Test, Balderstone was not picked again for England.

By the time he retired from cricket in 1986, Balderstone had played 390 first-class matches, had scored a total of 19,034 runs at an average of 34.11, including 32 centuries and a highest score of 181 not out and had taken 310 wickets at an average of 26.32, with a best bowling analysis of six for 25.

After retiring from cricket, Balderstone became an umpire. He died in 2000 from prostate cancer at the age of 59.

9. Leslie Balfour-Melville (1854-1937), *Scottish rugby player, cricketer, tennis player and golfer*

Leslie Balfour-Melville was born in Edinburgh in 1854.

Balfour-Melville both represented Scotland in more than one sport and was Scottish champion in other sports. His first cap was awarded to him in 1872 when he was picked whilst still a schoolboy at the age of 17 to play for Scotland at full-back against England in his one and only rugby international, a game which was won by England two goals to one.

Two years later, Balfour-Melville played his first game of cricket for Scotland and continued playing for them until 1910 – his last match was against Ireland in 1910, when he was 56 years old. He won a total of 18 caps at cricket for Scotland, his proudest moment being in 1882 when, as opening bat and wicketkeeper, he captained Scotland to a famous eight wicket victory over the touring Australian team – Balfour-Melville was Scotland's top scorer with 73 runs. One of his sons, James, also won two caps at cricket for Scotland, in 1913, before losing his life in the First World War.

By 1879, Balfour-Melville had become Scottish tennis champion and, in the 1880s, became Scotland's billiards champion. By the end of the 1880s, he was enjoying success at golf. Between 1886 and 1920, he played in the British Amateur Golf Championships, winning it in 1895 after having been runner-up in 1889; he played three times in the British Open, his best result being in 1888 when he was the leading amateur and finished in fifth place. In 1902, he represented Scotland in their first international match, against England; in 1906, he was appointed Captain of the Royal and Ancient Golf Club and, in 1910, was runner-up in the French Amateur Championships.

After his playing days were over, Balfour-Melville was appointed President of the Scottish Rugby Union and President of the Scottish Cricket Union.

Balfour-Melville died in 1937, aged 83.

10. Suzie Bates (1987-), *New Zealand cricketer and basketball player*

Suzie Bates was born in Dunedin, New Zealand in 1987.

Bates is a cricketer who bats right-handed and bowls right-arm medium pace. She has been playing cricket for Otago since 2002 and for New Zealand since 2006, when she made her one day international debut. Since then, up to New Zealand's tour to India at the end of June 2015, she has played in 71 ODIs and in 70 Twenty20 internationals for New Zealand; in her ODIs, she has scored 2,328 runs at an average of 36.95 with six centuries and a highest score of 168 and taken 52 wickets at an average of 31.13 with best bowling figures of 4 for 7. In her 70 Twenty20 matches, she has scored 1,664 runs at an average of 25.21 with a top score of 94 not out and taken 38 wickets at 21.28 apiece, with best figures of four for 26.

In 2013, Bates was named the Women's ODI Cricketer of the Year and Player of the Tournament at the ICC World Cup. A year later, she was selected to captain a World XI in a match against England at Lord's.

Bates has also represented New Zealand at basketball and played for them at the 2008 Olympics in Beijing, where New Zealand took tenth place.

11. Grahame Bilby (1941-   ), *New Zealand criceter and footballer*

Grahame Bilby was born in Wellington, New Zealand in 1941.

Bilby played cricket for Wellington from 1962 until 1977 and, after scoring 161 against Otago in 1964, was picked to open the batting against the touring England team in the first two Tests; in his four Test innings, he only scored 55 runs at an average of 13.75 with a top score of 28 and, after being unavailable for the third Test through injury, was not selected again.

By the time he retired from cricket, he had played 57 games of first-class cricket, scoring 2,936 runs at an average of 32.62 with three centuries and his 161 against Otago in 1964 being his highest score; he rarely bowled but did end his career with one wicket to his name, which cost him 34 runs.

Bilby also played football for New Zealand as an inside-forward. He played a total of 27 games of football for New Zealand between 1967 and 1971, including an evening game when he had been playing cricket for Wellington during the day. Of his 27 games for New Zealand, eight were against international opposition, against whom he scored just the one goal and two were World Cup qualifiers against Israel in 1970, both of which Israel won.

Away from sport, Bilby worked in IT until his retirement.

12. Reginald Birkett (1849-1898), *English footballer and rugby player*

Reginald Birkett was born in London in 1849.

In 1871, Birkett was not only present at the meeting in Regent Street, London at which the Rugby Football Union was formed but also became one of its original 13 committee members. The same year he played for England against Scotland in the first ever rugby international and scored England's first ever try; however, on account of the fact that points were only awarded for tries if they were converted, Scotland won the match 1-0 by virtue of one of their tries being converted and Birkett's try not being converted.

Birkett was also a keen footballer and played in goal for Clapham Rovers in the F. A. Cup Final in 1879 when they lost to Old Etonians 1-0; a week later, he was selected to play for England against Scotland and, despite letting in four goals, ended up on the winning side with England winning 5-4.

Birkett did not play for England again but he did appear in another F. A. Cup Final for Clapham Rovers when they won the 1880 final 1-0 against Oxford University.

Birkett's brother, Louis, also played rugby for England, as did his son John.

Birkett died in 1898 at the age of 49, following an accident at home; whilst suffering from diphtheria, he leapt from a window while being helped into his bed and fell 20 feet to his death – at the inquest, a verdict of suicide whilst delirious was returned.

13. Vsevolod Bobrov (1922-1979), *Russian footballer and ice hockey player*

Vsevelod Bobrov was born in 1922 in Morshansk, Russia.

Whilst serving in the Soviet army during the Second World War, Bobrov played bandy, an outdoor game that can be described as being similar to field hockey played on ice; after the War, Bobrov joined the Army football club CSKA Moscow and, in 1945, was loaned to Dynamo Moscow for their tour to England and Scotland. Bobrov's football career continued until 1953 by which time he had played 115 games at club level, in which he scored a total of 99 goals. He also was picked for the USSR team which competed in the 1952 Olympics, playing in all three of their games; in these games, Bobrov scored five goals including a hat-trick against the eventual silver medallists Yugoslavia in a memorable 5-5 draw, after Yugoslavia had led 5-1 with only 15 minutes left to play.

A year after Bobrov joined CSKA Moscow, he started playing ice hockey, which he continued to play until 1957. He played a total of 130 games for the Soviet team, scoring a total of 254 goals and was a member of the Soviet team which won the World Championships in 1954 and 1956 and were runners-up in 1955 and 1957, as well as the team which won the gold medal at the 1956 Winter Olympics; four years before winning the World Championships in 1954, almost all the Soviet ice hockey team died in a plane crash, something Bobrov had avoided as he had been travelling by train instead.

Bobrov died in 1979 at the age of 57. After his death, he was chosen as Russia's third greatest athlete of the 20th century.

14. Brian Booth (1933-), *Australian cricketer and hockey player*

Brian Booth was born near Bathurst, New South Wales in 1933.

Booth was first selected to play cricket for New South Wales in 1955 and, later on that season, was selected to play against the touring England team. After missing a season to concentrate on his hockey and participation in the 1956 Olympics, his success as a right-hand batsman earned him a place in the Australian team touring England in 1961. In the next Ashes series, in 1962/63 when England were touring Australia, he scored two centuries; he followed this up with two more centuries in the summer of 1963, against the visitors South Africa, for which he was named Australia's cricketer of the year.

Booth's last appearances for Australia were when England toured in 1965/66. He captained in two of the Tests on this tour in place of the regular captain Bobby Simpson, who was absent from the first Test due to injury (a broken wrist) and from the third Test due to illness (chickenpox). The third Test proved to be Booth's last, with Australia losing the Test by an innings and 93 runs; poor form led to Booth being dropped but he at least had the consolation of receiving a letter from Don Bradman, one of the selectors, expressing his regret at Booth's omission.

By the time he had retired, Booth had played in 29 Tests for Australia; he scored a total of 1,773 runs at an average of 42.21. He scored five centuries, with a top score of 169 not out. His occasional bowling brought him three Test wickets at an average of 48.66.

Booth's first-class cricket career continued until 1968. In all, he played in 183 games of first-class cricket, scoring 11,265 runs, including 26 centuries and a top score of 214 not out, at an average of 45.42; he also took 16 first-class wickets at an average of 59.75. Years after his retirement from cricket, the cricket writer E. W. Stanton summarised Booth as "that model of a man and of a batsman who tends to be under-rated and forgotten because both he and his cricket were so blamelessly self-effacing".

Before being selected to play cricket for Australia, Booth played hockey in the Australian winter and was picked as a member of the Australian team for their home Olympics in 1956. Although he did not play in any of the group stage games, he was selected in two matches, one against Belgium (which was drawn 2-2) and one against New Zealand (which Australia won 1-0), matches which determined the final places at the Games.

After his sporting career ended, Booth became a schoolmaster and Anglican lay preacher. In 1988, he was awarded the MBE for services to the community and sport; his religious beliefs have led him to write about sportsmanship in sport and the Australian edition of the 2002 Wisden Cricketers' Almanack published an article by him titled "The Curse of Sledging", something of which he does not approve.

15. Norman Borrett (1917-2004), *English hockey player, squash player and cricketer*

Norman Borrett was born in 1917, in Wanstead, London.

After leaving Framlingham College, where he had been captain of hockey, cricket, squash, fives, athletics and swimming, Borrett went up to Cambridge University where he won a blue at both hockey and squash, captaining the university in both sports. He also played in the Cambridge Seniors cricket match, which was considered an important university trial fixture and in which he took a hat-trick but he was not picked for the University team despite representing Essex during his time at Cambridge.

At squash, Borrett was British Amateur Champion five years in a row, from 1946 to 1950, winning each final without losing a game; he was expected to make it six in a row but for his withdrawal from the 1951 Championships due to food poisoning. He also represented England at squash, playing for them 11 times and captaining them in most of these matches.

Borrett also captained England and Great Britain at hockey. He played a total of 30 games for England, captaining them in 11 matches and a total of seven games for Great Britain, including five games at the 1948 Olympics in which he scored 10 goals (six of them against the USA in an 11-0 victory and four of them against Afghanistan in an 8-0 victory) and captained them to the silver medal.

As well as playing cricket for Essex in two games in 1939, whilst at university, Borrett also played for them in one game after the Second World War, in 1946; in his three games for Essex, he scored 33 runs at an average of 16.5 but took no wickets in his 16 overs which cost 43 runs. In 1947, he started playing for Devon in the Minor Counties Championship and, over the next 11 years, played for them on 50 occasions, scoring a total of 2,408 runs at an average of over 36.

As well as excelling at squash and hockey and playing first-class cricket, Borrett played golf off a handicap of 4, was good enough to qualify to play tennis at Wimbledon (but claimed he was too busy to enter) and declined an invitation to co-drive in the 24 Hour Le Mans race.

After the War, Borrett became a schoolmaster, returning to his old school in 1950. He died in 2004 at the age of 87; in his obituary in The Times, it was said of him that he was "probably Britain's most talented post-War all-round sportsman".

16. Ian Botham (1957-   ), *English cricketer and footballer*

Sir Ian Botham was born in Heswall, in the Wirral, in 1955.

Botham played first-class cricket from 1974 until 1993, first with Somerset (from 1974 until 1986), then with Worcestershire (from 1987 until 1991) and finally with Durham (in 1992 and 1993); he also played for Queensland in 1987 and 1988.

He was first selected to play for England in 1977 and, in his 102 Tests for England, proved himself to be one of the greatest all-rounders of all time. He scored a total of 5,200 runs in Tests, at an average of 33.54, including 14 centuries and a top score of 208; he took 383 wickets (a record for an English cricketer until overtaken by Jimmy Anderson in April 2015), at an average of 28.40 and held on to 120 catches (prior to the Ashes series in 2015, only one less than the most by an Englishman). On 27 occasions, he took five wickets in an innings, his best return being eight for 34 against Pakistan at Lord's in 1978 and, on four occasions, took 10 or more wickets in a match, his best return being 13 wickets for 106 against India in the Golden Jubilee Test in Mumbai in 1980; just for good measure, Botham also scored 114 in the first innings of that match, a match England won by 10 wickets.

Botham also played in 116 one day internationals for England, scoring a total of 2,113 runs at an average of 23.21 and with a top score of 79 and taking 145 wickets at an average of 28.54. In all first-class matches, he scored 19,399 runs, including 38 centuries and a top score of 228, averaging 33.97 with the bat and took 1,172 wickets, averaging 27.22 with the ball.

Botham's statistics though do not tell the whole story. On numerous occasions, he produced match-winning performances and none more so than during the 1981 Ashes series. Having been dismissed for "a pair" in the Lord's Test following which he resigned as captain, he turned in three outstanding performances in the remaining four Tests of the series to turn a 1-0 deficit into a 3-1 victory; in the third Test, he scored a remarkable 149 not out in a match England won despite following on; in the fourth Test, he took the last five Australian wickets for one run, a match England won by 29 runs; and in the fifth Test, he scored 118 runs in an innings of only 102 balls lasting a little over two hours and including six 6s and thirteen 4s. On the back of these performances, Botham was the BBC's Sports Personality of the Year in 1981.

Botham also played professional football. He first joined Yeovil Town in 1978 before they attained Football League status and played centre-half for them in 17 games over the next two seasons. In 1980, he joined Scunthorpe United and over the next five years played 11 games for them. He is one of three Scunthorpe footballers who went on to achieve greater things and captain their countries, albeit in the case of Botham not at football - the other two are the England footballers Kevin Keegan and Ray Clemence.

Botham is also a keen golfer with a handicap of seven. One of his more memorable feats on the golf course is to drive the 301 yard 10th at the Belfry, although, by three-putting, he did not manage to birdie or eagle the hole.

Botham has also undertaken a number of charity walks for leukaemia; his first was back in 1985 when he walked from John O'Groats to Land's End; to date, he has raised over £12 million and, in 2007, was knighted for his services to charity. Botham has also been, for a number of years, a regular member of the Sky Sports cricket commentary team.

17. Freddie Brooks (1883-1947), *Rhodesian cricketer, rugby player, tennis player and athlete*

Freddie Brooks was born in Mumbai (then Bombay) in 1883.

Brooks was educated at Bedford School in England and, as a schoolboy, was the public schools' champion in the 100 yards, the 110 yard hurdles, the long jump and the high jump.

After leaving school, he emigrated to Rhodesia, having been offered a civil service job by the then Administrator of Rhodesia, William Milton (see Chapter 95); in 1905, Brooks played for Rhodesia in their inaugural Currie Cup cricket match against Transvaal, top-scoring in the first innings with a score of 61. A year later, he was representing Rhodesia at rugby in South Africa's Currie Cup. Although he failed to meet the five year residential qualifications required for selection for the touring Springboks to England in 1906/07, he was invited to join the touring party and, whilst in England, played for Bedford. His performances with Bedford led to his selection in the South v. North fixture, which was seen as an England trial. In this match he scored four tries following which he was selected to play for England against the touring South Africa team, the team with whom he had travelled to England in the first place; Brooks scored England's only points with a try, in a 3-3 draw.

Back in Rhodesia, Brooks only played one more game of first-class cricket for Rhodesia, in 1910, by which time he had also won the Rhodesian tennis title and held the national long jump title.

Brooks's work in the civil service earned him an OBE; he died in 1947 at the age of 64.

18. Carol Bryant (1947-), *English Paralympian athlete, table-tennis player, fencer, swimmer and basketball player*

Carol Bryant (now better known as Caz Walton) was born in 1947.

Bryant has represented Great Britain at five Paralympic Games. She first appeared at the Games in Tokyo in 1964 where she won gold medals in both the athletics events she entered. Four years later, she won two more gold medals in athletics as well as her first gold medal at table-tennis. The 1972 Games proved even more successful, when she went one better than in 1968, by winning a gold in fencing as well as another two in athletics and another one in table-tennis. Her next, and last, gold medal came at the 1988 Games when she won her second gold medal in fencing.

Although she only won gold medals in three different sports at the Paralympic Games, Bryant also competed in swimming events, winning a silver medal in 1968 and a bronze medal in 1972. At the 1988 Games, she was also a member of the Great Britain basketball team but failed to add basketball as a fifth medal-winning sport to the four in which she had already won medals.

Bryant's 10 gold medals at the Paralympic Games make her Great Britain's second most successful female Paralympian in terms of gold medals, behind Tanni Grey-Thompson. However, when winning the bronze medal in the Women's Incomplete Class Pentathlon Event in 1968, her total points score of 2,487, which left her in third place, did not include the 639 points she scored in the 50 metre swim event – had it done so, she would have won the gold medal, which in turn would have given her the same number of gold medals as Grey-Thompson.

In 1970, Bryant was awarded the Bill McGowran Trophy for Disabled Sports Personality of the Year by the Sports Journalists Association and, in 2010, an OBE for services to disability sport.

19. Maria Canins (1949-), *Italian skier and cyclist*

Maria Canins was born in the Dolomite region of Italy in 1949.

Between 1971 and 1985, Canins was Italy's cross-country skiing champion on 13 occasions, over distances of 5km, 10km and 20km and, for 10 years in a row from 1979 to 1988, she won the Marcialonga, a 70km cross-country ski race hosted in Trentino, Italy.

As well as being a national cross-country skiing champion, Canins was also a champion cyclist. Between 1982 and 1989, she won the silver medal twice and the bronze medal twice in the UCI Road World Championships; she represented Italy in cycling events at the Summer Olympics in 1984 (when she came fifth in the Women's Individual Road Race) and 1988 (when she came 32nd in the Women's Individual Road Race). In 1985, Canins won the Grande Boucle (the female version of the Tour de France), a title she retained the following year – on three other occasions, she was runner-up. She also won the Giro d'Italie Femminile (the female version of the Giro d'Italie) in 1988.

By the 1990s, Canins had turned her attention to mountain biking and, in 1996 and 1996, was world champion.

20. Bill Carson (1916-1944), *New Zealand cricketer and rugby player*

William Nicol Carson was born in Gisborne, New Zealand in 1916.

Carson played his first game of cricket for Auckland in 1936 and, in his second match for Auckland, in only his second innings in first-class cricket, scored 290 against Otago; his partnership of 445 with Paul Whitelaw was, at the time, the world record for a third wicket partnership in first-class cricket, a record which lasted until 1975. In his next match, against Wellington, he scored 194.

Carson's performances led to him being selected for the New Zealand team to tour England in 1937 and, although he played 24 matches on the tour, 20 of which were first-class matches, he was not picked to play in any of the Test matches.

On his return to New Zealand, Carson chose to concentrate on his rugby; by then he had played 31 games of first-class cricket, scoring 1,535 runs at an average of 34.88 and taking 35 wickets with his left-arm fast medium bowling at an average of 21.48; he only added two more centuries to the two he had scored in his first three matches and his 290 remained his highest score.

At rugby, Carson played as a flanker and, in 1938, was picked to play for the All Blacks against the Combined Western Districts; he followed this up with two appearances in an All Black shirt on their tour to Australia where he played against Newcastle and the ACT but, as with his cricket, was not selected to play in any Test matches.

War broke out a year after the tour to Australia and Carson served with the New Zealand Artillery, seeing action in Crete, North Africa and Italy. He was awarded the Military Cross in 1943 whilst in North Africa for quickly positioning his guns to fire accurately against two well-equipped Italian battalions at the battle of Mareth. A year later, whilst in Italy, in 1944, he was wounded and, after contracting jaundice at Bari, died at the age of 28 on board a boat taking him to Egypt, en route to New Zealand.

21. Ric Charlesworth (1952-   ), *Australian hockey player and cricketer*

Ric Charlesworth was born in Western Australia in 1952.

Charlesworth played 47 games of first-class cricket for Western Australia between 1972 and 1979, in which he scored 2,327 runs, with a top score of 101 not out (his only century), at an average of 30.22. He was a member of the Western Australia Sheffield Shield winning team on three occasions.

Charlesworth was also an international hockey player; he represented Australia at the Olympic Games in 1972, 1976 (when Australia won the silver medal), in 1984 (when he was captain) and in 1988 – he was also selected to captain the hockey team at the 1980 Olympics in Moscow, but they were boycotted by Australia. He also represented Australia at hockey in other international competitions, including in the Hockey World Cup in 1986 when he was a member of Australia's winning team.

Charlesworth retired from international hockey following the 1988 Olympics, having played 227 games for Australia.

After his retirement as a player, Charlesworth was elected as the Federal member for Perth representing Australia's Labor party; he stayed in politics as a Member of Parliament for 10 years before stepping down in 1993.

Since retiring from politics, Charlesworth has been coach to the Australian women's and men's hockey teams, both of which have had even more than success with him as their coach than he did as a player; with Charlesworth coaching the women's team, Australia won the World Cup in 1994 and 1996 and the Olympic gold medal in 1996 and 2000 and, with him coaching the men's team, Australia won the World Cup in 2010 and 2014, after which he resigned as coach.

22. Eddie Charlton (1929-2004), *Australian billiards and snooker player, surfer and Australian Rules footballer*

Eddie Charlton was born in Merewether, New South Wales in 1929.

Charlton played First Division Aussie Rules football for 10 years and was a member of the Swansea-Belmont team which won the Australian Surfing Championships in 1950 before he became a professional billiards player and snooker player in 1963. From 1964 until 1984, Charlton was the Australian billiards champion 20 times, missing out in only one year and, on three occasions, was runner-up in the World Billiards Championships.

Charlton was also runner-up three times in the World Snooker Championships but had more success on BBC's Pot Black, which he won three times.

Other sports Charlton competed in included speed roller-skating, cricket and boxing but one of his proudest moments was when he carried the Olympic Torch on its way to the opening ceremony at the 1956 Olympics in Melbourne.

Charlton died in 2004 at the age of 75.

23. Mike Cleary (1940-), *Australian rugby player and athlete*

Michael Cleary was born in Randwick, New South Wales in 1940.

Cleary joined the Randwick rugby union club in 1959 and, by 1961, was selected to play on the wing for Australia; his first three Tests were against the touring Fijians and he scored a try on debut in a 24-6 victory and two tries in his second Test in a 20-14 victory; the third Test against Fiji was drawn 3-3. Cleary was then selected for the tour to South Africa; both matches on the tour were lost by Australia but Cleary had the consolation of scoring Australia's only try in the second Test which was lost 23-11. Cleary's sixth and final Test as a rugby union player came later that year against France, which France won 15-8.

In 1962, Cleary switched codes and joined the rugby league side South Sydney Rabbitohs, but initially retained his amateur status to allow him to compete in the 1962 Commonwealth Games, where he took the bronze medal in the 100 yards event with a time of 9.78 seconds, which was outside his fastest recorded time of 9.3 seconds.

Within his first year as a league player, Cleary was chosen to play for the national side and, over the next eight years, appeared for the Australian team in eight Tests, scoring five tries. As well as playing in eight Tests and playing in non-Test matches on the tour to Britain in 1963, Cleary also played 11 games for New South Wales and 140 games for South Sydney Rabbitohs, winning the premiership three times, in 1967, 1968 and 1970, before joining Eastern Suburb Roosters in 1971.

After a season with the Roosters, Cleary retired from professional sport. Cleary then entered the world of politics and, from 1981 until 1988, was New South Wales's Minister for Sport and Tourism under the Labor Government.

24. Brian Close (1931-   ), *English cricketer and footballer*

Brian Close was born in 1931, in Rawdon, Yorkshire.

Close played cricket for Yorkshire from 1949 until 1970 and ended his cricket career with Somerset for whom he played from 1971 until 1977. Whilst at Yorkshire, he captained them to four championship titles and, whilst at Somerset, he had under his wing two young players starting out on their cricket careers, namely Ian Botham and Viv Richards (see Chapters 16 and 119): Close is given much credit for moulding them into the successful cricketers they became.

In his first year at Yorkshire, Close was also selected to play for England in the third Test against the touring New Zealand team, making him, at the age of 18 years and 149 days, the youngest cricketer ever to play for England. Close was still playing for England 27 years later when he was recalled to the team to take on the pace attack of the West Indians, which included Andy Roberts and Michael Holding.

Although his Test career spanned 27 years, he only played in 22 Tests, captaining England in seven of them - in the Tests Close captained, England won six of them and drew the other. In his 22 Tests, he scored 887 runs at an average of 25.34 with a highest score of 70 and took 18 wickets at an average of 29.55. His record in first-class career was better; in his 786 matches, he scored 34,994 runs at an average of 33.26 and took 1,171 wickets at an average of 26.42, with a personal best of eight for 41; he scored 52 centuries, with a top score of 198 and his reputation as a fearless fielder brought him 813 catches – only nine cricketers have played more first-class matches and only four outfielders have taken more catches than him.

As well as being a cricketer, Close had also played football until injuries and cricket forced him to give it up. He signed as an amateur for Leeds United at the age of 14 before turning professional with them at the age of 18. In 1948, he became the first Leeds United player to be picked for the England youth team when he played in a match against Scotland. In 1950, he signed for Arsenal before moving to Bradford City in 1952. Although he did not play in any league fixtures for Leeds or Arsenal, he did play in six games for Bradford City in which he scored two goals for them.

In 1972, Close was awarded the CBE for his services to cricket; since retiring as a player, Close has been an England selector and a member of the Yorkshire committee, as well as helping with the development of young Yorkshire cricketers.

25. Denis Compton (1918-1997), *English cricketer and footballer*

Denis Compton was born in Hendon, London in 1918.

During his career as a professional cricketer, Compton broke a number of records, some of which still stand today but his success as a cricketer did not prevent his enjoying success on the football field with Arsenal as well.

Compton was a right-handed batsman and left-arm "chinaman" bowler who first played for Middlesex in 1936. His Test debut followed a year later and, by the time of his retirement from Test cricket in 1957, he had played in 78 Tests, scoring a total of 5,807 runs, including 17 centuries and a top score of 278, at an average of 50.06; he had also taken 25 wickets at an average of 56.40; but for the War, he would no doubt have played in a number more Tests.

He continued playing first-class career, mostly for Middlesex, until 1964. During this time, in all first-class cricket, he played 515 matches, scoring 38,982 runs at an average of 51.85 and taking 622 wickets at an average of 32.27. His runs total is the 21st highest of all time and his 123 centuries the 12th highest of all time. His centuries include the 18 he scored in 1947 (the most in any season), the year in which he was the leading batsman, both in terms of runs scored and overall average; they also include a 300, which he scored in 181 minutes in 1948 for the MCC against North Eastern Transvaal, which remains, in terms of time, the fastest triple century of all time.

In his book "The Top 100 Cricketers Of All Time", which was first published in 2009, Christopher Martin-Jenkins ranked Compton number 21 whilst David Gower, in his book "David Gower's 50 Greatest Cricketers Of All Time", first published in 2015, ranked Compton one higher at number 20; and, in Wisden's survey of those whose excellence at cricket during the 20th century made the greatest contribution to the game, Compton came ninth.

Compton also made his debut for Arsenal in 1936, playing left-wing in a 2-2 draw with Derby County in which he scored one of the goals. When Arsenal won the league division 1 (then the top league) in 1937/38, he made seven league appearances for them and, when they won it again in the 1947/48 season, he played in 14 of their games. Injuries restricted the number of appearances he made for Arsenal but 1950 saw him pick up an F. A. Cup Winners medal with Arsenal, when he played in the final in Arsenal's 2-0 win over Liverpool. Compton played a total of 60 games for Arsenal and scored 16 goals for them.

Despite being stationed in India during the War, this did not prevent Compton playing for Arsenal during this period in 120 wartime games, in which he scored 74 goals; he was also selected to represent England in 12 wartime and Victory matches, but none of these rank as official international matches.

After retiring from cricket, Compton's popularity meant there were plenty of job opportunities for him; he became a television commentator and newspaper columnist, as well as working for advertising agencies, having been during his cricketing days in the early 1950s the Brylcream Boy in their advertising campaign. Compton also served two terms as President of Middlesex CCC.

Compton was awarded the CBE in 1958. He died from septicaemia in 1997; since his death, his grandson Nick has played cricket for England in nine Test matches.

To write about Compton just in terms of statistics do not do him or his achievements justice. Much has been written about him – E. W. Stanton wrote that he doubted if any game at any period had thrown up anyone to match Compton's popular appeal in the England of 1947 to 1949. In his obituary in Wisden 1988, the exuberance of his batting and personality was credited with being a symbol of national revival after the War, the obituary concluding that "cricket was hugely fortunate that such a gifted sportsman graced the game with his presence. It was doubly blessed that he was a man of modesty, charm and good nature."

26. Leslie Compton (1912-1984), *English footballer and cricketer*

Leslie Compton was born in Woodford, Essex in 1912, the older brother of Denis Compton (see Chapter 25).

Like his younger brother, Compton played first-class cricket for Middlesex and football for Arsenal and although Denis was the more accomplished cricketer, Leslie was the more accomplished footballer.

His football career with Arsenal started in 1930 and continued until 1952, by which time he had played 273 games for them, including 253 in the league; he started as a full-back and then moved to centre-half; as a defender, scoring goals was a bit of a rarity but, over his career, he did manage to score six times for his club.

In the 1947/48 season, Compton was a member of the league winning team and, in 1950, in the F. A. Cup winning team, alongside his brother; in the semi-final, Compton headed a last-minute equaliser from a corner taken by Denis to keep Arsenal in the Cup. 1950 also saw him selected to play football for England at the age of 38 years and 64 days, making him the oldest outfield player ever on his debut for England. His first international was against Wales in the British Championships, where he played at centre-half, alongside future England manager Alf Ramsey, in a 4-2 victory. His second and only other international was a week later, a friendly against Yugoslavia, which was drawn 2-2 but a game in which Compton was unfortunate enough to score an own goal.

Compton's cricket career with Middlesex started in 1938. The early part of his cricketing days with Middlesex was interrupted by the War but, by the time he retired in 1956, he had played a total of 272 games for them, as well as representing the MCC in 1947. He finished his career with 5,814 runs at an average of 16.8 and one century to his name, a score of 107; his occasional bowling brought him 12 wickets at an average of 47.41 but his primary role in the Middlesex team was as wicketkeeper and when he retired, he had taken 470 catches and made 129 stumpings.

In winning the County Championship in 1947 and the football league in the 1947/48 season, Compton became, with his brother, the only brothers ever to have won the national titles at both football and cricket.

After his retirement from cricket in 1956, Compton ran a pub in North London. He died in 1984 at the age of 72.

27. Lionel Conacher (1900-1954), *Canadian wrestler, boxer, American footballer, ice hockey player, baseball player and lacrosse player*

Lionel Conacher was born in Toronto in 1900.

By the age of 16, Conacher had become Ontario's lightweight wrestling champion and, by the time he had turned 20, had become Canada's light-heavyweight boxing champion. In 1921, he took on, and was knocked out by, world heavyweight boxing champion Jack Dempsey, in an exhibition match. 1921 was also the year Conacher won the Grey Cup as a member of the Toronto Argonauts Canadian Football team.

Conacher's strength and speed – he ran 100 yards in under 10 seconds – were suited not only to American/Canadian football but also to lacrosse and, in 1922, Conacher helped Toronto win the Ontario Lacrosse Association senior title.

By 1925, Conacher was playing ice hockey in the NHL; over an ice hockey career spanning 13 seasons, he played a total of 494 games, 43 for the

Pittsburgh Pirates, 143 for the New York Americans, 48 for the Chicago Black Hawks and 260 for the Montreal Maroons. Twice he won the Stanley Cup, first with the Chicago Black Hawks in 1934 and then the following year with the Montreal Maroons. Only one other sportsman, Carl Voss (see Chapter 159), has won both the Grey Cup and the Stanley Cup.

Conacher also turned his hand to baseball and, in 1926, won the International League Championship with the Toronto Maple Leafs.

In 1931, Conacher played for the Montreal Maroons in a form of lacrosse which was played in ice hockey arenas which would otherwise have been unused.

Conacher retired from professional sport in 1937, by which time he had been a champion in five different sports; he then entered the world of politics, eventually winning a seat in the House of Commons in 1949. Two days after his 54th birthday, whilst playing in a softball match between MPs and members of the parliamentary press gallery, Conacher died of a heart attack after sprinting to third base. After his death, he was voted Canada's top athlete of the first half of the 20th century.

28. Frank Conner (1946-), *American golfer and tennis player*

Frank Conner was born in 1946, in Vienna where his father, serving in the US Forces, was posted.

Conner was the US National Junior tennis champion in 1963 and took part in the last three US Open tennis championships of the amateur era. In 1965 and 1966, he failed to get beyond the first round, although, in 1965, he lost to fellow American Jim Osborne who was beaten two rounds later by the eventual winner, Manuel Santana; Conner fared slightly better in 1967 by making it to the second round, where he lost to the Australian Ray Keldie.

Believing he could earn more money as a golfer, Conner gave up tennis and took up golf, turning professional in 1971. By 1975, he had joined the PGA tour which he played on until 1989 and again in 1992. During his golf career, he won seven tournaments and played in each of the four majors; although he never made the cut at either the Masters or the British Open, his best performance at the US PGA was tied 23rd place and at the US Open, tied 6th place, where he ended seven shots behind the winner, the Australian David Graham – also tied with Conner in 6th place was Jack Nicklaus.

After turning 50, Conner joined the PGA Senior Tour, which he played on for seven years, his best results being twice finishing in second place.

Conner remains one of only two sportsmen to have competed in the US Open at both tennis and golf, the other one being Ellsworth Vines (see Chapter 158); more recently, the American Mardy Fish attempted to emulate Conner and Vines, when trying, but failing, to qualify for the 2015 US Open at golf, having retired from tennis two years earlier; Fish was ranked number 7 in the world at tennis in 2011 and, during his tennis career, reached the quarter-finals of three of the four majors, including the US Open.

29. Mike Corby (1940-   ), *English hockey player, squash player and tennis player*

Mike Corby was born in 1940.

Whilst at Mill Hill School, Corby played hockey for England schoolboys, won the British Junior Hard Court Championships at Wimbledon and won the Drysdale Cup, the Under-19 boys' competition at squash.

After leaving school, Corby concentrated on his hockey and his squash. In total, he played over 100 games of hockey for England and Great Britain, including representing Great Britain at the 1964 Olympics and the 1972 Olympics – he was not selected for the 1968 Olympics because of his squash commitments. At the 1964 Games, Great Britain finished in ninth equal place and eight years later finished in fifth place – a defeat against

New Zealand when fielding a weakened side in a group stage game may have cost them the bronze medal.

At squash, Corby achieved a highest ranking of number 5 in the world. For eight years, he was England's number 1 amateur squash player and he competed in the world championships in 1967 and 1971.

His performances as a sportsman earned Corby the title "Corinthian of the Century", as voted by readers of The Sunday Times. Since retiring as a player, Corby has been heavily involved in sports administration, having taken on the roles of Vice-President of the World Squash Federation and President of the English Hockey Association; he also been heavily involved with the successful development and growth of fitness centres and clubs in England.

30. Leonard Crawley (1903-1981), *English golfer and cricketer*

Leonard Crawley was born in 1903, in Nacton, Suffolk.

Crawley was a leading amateur golfer, who won the English Amateur Championships in 1931 and was runner-up in 1934 and 1937. He played for Great Britain and Ireland in the Walker Cup against America in 1932, 1934, 1938 and 1947. As an Oxford University blue at golf, he played in the President's Putter, winning it on four occasions.

Crawley was also a cricketer, scoring a century at Lord's for Harrow in the 1921 fixture against Eton; four years later, he missed out on another century at Lord's, when scoring 98 in the Varsity Match. As well as playing golf and cricket for Oxford University, he also played first pair for them at rackets. Crawley played first-class cricket from 1922 until 1939, playing a total of 109 first-class games, in which he scored 5,227 runs at an average of 31.11, with eight centuries and a top score of 222; the 17 overs he bowled brought him no wickets and conceded 57 runs. His 109 first-class games included eight for the MCC on its tour to the West Indies in 1926, two years before the West Indies were granted Test status.

In 1932, Crawley was asked about his availability for the Ashes tour that winter to Australia; because of his selection for the Walker Cup, he declared himself unavailable to tour on what became known as the Bodyline Series.

As well as being a golfer and cricketer, Crawley was more than competent at a number of other sports, including tennis, rackets, ice-skating and shooting.

Later in life, Crawley worked as the golfing correspondent for The Daily Telegraph.

Crawley died in 1981 at the age of 77.

31. Graham Cross (1943-), *English cricketer and footballer*

Graham Cross was born in Leicester in 1943.

Cross first played football for Leicester City in 1960 and by the time he left them in 1976, had played 599 games for them; he started his career as an inside-forward but ended up as a centre-half. During his time at Leicester, he was capped a record 11 times for the England Under 23 team and appeared in two F. A. Cup Finals (1963 and 1969) and two League Cup Finals (1964 and 1965) – only on one occasion though did he pick up a winners' medal, the 1964 League Cup. After leaving Leicester, he made a further 122 league appearances, for Chesterfield, Brighton & Hove Albion, Preston North End and Lincoln City, before retiring in 1977.

Cross also played cricket for Leicestershire, making his debut in 1962. He continued to play for them until 1976 and, although he only played in 83 first-class matches for them over this period, he did play for them when they won the Benson & Hedges Cup in 1975, making him the only man to have played in cup finals at both Wembley and Lord's. His overall first-class cricket record in his 83 matches was 2,079 runs scored at an average of 18.39 with a highest score of 78 and 92 wickets at an average of 29.95 with best figures of four for 28.

32. Jim Cumbes (1944-), *English footballer and cricketer*

Jim Cumbes was born in 1944 in East Didsbury, Manchester.

Cumbes remains one of the last sportsmen who combined a career as a professional cricketer in the summer with a professional football career over the winter months.

His cricket career started at Lancashire for whom he played from 1963 until 1967; he then spent three years at Surrey before moving back to Lancashire for a brief spell in 1971 and then on to Worcestershire, where he stayed until 1981; he spent his final year as a cricketer at Warwickshire. Over his 20 year career, he played in 161 first-class matches. Picked as a fast-medium bowler, he had little success with the bat, scoring 498 runs at an average of 7.54, with a top score of 43; however, his bowling brought him 379 wickets at an average of 30.20 and a best return of six for 24.

Cumbes's career as a professional goalkeeper started with Tranmere Rovers in 1966; he played 137 games for them over four seasons before moving to West Bromwich Albion, where he spent two years playing 64 games for them. In 1971, he moved again, this time to Aston Villa, where he played 157 games for them over the next four years. Cumbes ended his football-playing days in North America.

After retiring as a professional sportsman, Cumbes was the chief executive at Lancashire County Cricket Club from 1998 until 2012.

33. Ces Dacre (1899-1975), *New Zealand cricketer and footballer*

Charles Christian Ralph Dacre (known as Ces Dacre) was born in Auckland in 1899.

Dacre played his first game of first-class cricket for Auckland on Christmas Day in 1914 and his second on New Year's Day in 1915, but the First World War then put a hold on his cricket career until after it was over. However, the War did not put an end to Dacre's sporting activities; he played rugby union for the Railway Club until 1917 and then played rugby league when he and others from the Railway Club switched codes and formed Railway XIII.

After the War, Dacre switched codes again to play association football and, in 1922 and 1923, played in four international matches for New Zealand, in which he scored two goals. In 1926, he played in the final of the Chatham Cup (New Zealand's knockout competition) for North Side but ended up on the losing side.

By this time, Dacre had already resumed his cricket career, playing again for Auckland and towards the end of his career for Gloucestershire. Between 1914 and 1936, he played a total of 268 games of first-class cricket; as a right-handed batsman, he scored 12,223 runs at an average of 29.17, with 24 centuries to his name and a top score of 223 and, with his slow left-arm orthodox bowling, took 39 wickets at an average of 31.25, with best figures of five for 35.

Amongst his 268 games of first-class cricket were 37 he played for New Zealand before it was granted Test match status. He first played for New Zealand against the touring Australians in 1922; he toured Australia in 1925/26, playing in games against four of the Australian State teams and, in 1927, toured with the first New Zealand cricket team to visit England, where he played in 24 of their matches on tour. His last appearance for New Zealand was against New South Wales in 1927 when the New Zealanders were on the return journey of their England tour.

Dacre died in 1975 at the age of 76.

34. Eric Dalton (1906-1981), *South African cricketer and golfer*

Eric Dalton was born in Durban in 1906.

After only nine game of first-class cricket, Dalton was included in the South African team to tour England in 1929. Over the next 10 seasons,

Dalton played 15 Tests for South Africa, in which he scored 698 runs at an average of 31.72, with two centuries and a highest score of 117; his bowling brought him 12 wickets at an average of 40.83, two of his Test wickets being the wicket of Wally Hammond in the "timeless" Test in 1939, Hammond being stumped off Dalton's bowling in both innings.

In all first-class cricket, Dalton scored 5,333 runs at an average of 33.12 with a highest score of 157 and 13 centuries and took 139 wickets at an average of 25.81, with best bowling figures of six for 42.

After the Second World War, Dalton concentrated on his golf, a game he had taken up after being injured whilst playing cricket on tour to Australia in 1931/32 – Dalton had his jaw broken whilst facing Laurie Nash, who was on a hat-trick. In 1950, Dalton won South Africa's Amateur Championships and four years later represented South Africa at the first Commonwealth Tournament, held at St Andrews; that same year, he entered the British Amateur Championships, reaching the last 16.

Dalton died in 1981 at the age of 74.

35. A. B. de Villiers (1984-   ), *South African cricketer, rugby player, tennis player and badminton player*

Abraham Benjamin ("AB") de Villiers was born in Pretoria in 1984.

As a cricketer, de Villiers is one of the world's leading batsmen, who frequently keeps wicket and occasionally bowls. He made his Test match debut for South Africa in 2004, his ODI debut in 2005 and his Twenty20 debut in 2006.

In his 98 Tests up to South Africa's tour to Bangladesh at the beginning of July 2015 (which de Villiers was granted permission to miss on account of paternity leave), he has scored 7,606 runs at an average of 52.09, with 21 centuries and a highest score of 278 not out; and, in his 187 ODIs up to the end of the 2015 World Cup, he has scored 7,941 runs at an average of 53.65, with 20 centuries to his name and a highest score of 162 not out.

His batting has earned him the world's number one ranking in both Test cricket and one day cricket and, in one day cricket, he holds the record, in terms of balls received, for the fastest 50 (in 16 balls), the fastest 100 (in 31 balls) and the fastest 150 (in 66 balls) – the fastest 50 and the fastest 100 both came against the West Indies in an innings in which he faced only 44 balls before being finally dismissed for 149.

Before choosing cricket as his career, de Villiers excelled in a number of sports, achieving the following:

- being captain of South Africa's junior national rugby team
- holding six South African schools swimming records
- being shortlisted for junior national teams in both hockey and football
- holding the 100 metres sprint record in South African junior athletics
- being a member of South Africa's junior Davis Cup tennis team
- being the South African under-19 badminton champion

In addition to the above, de Villiers also has a scratch handicap at golf.

36. Sophie Devine (1989-   ), *New Zealand cricketer and hockey player*

Sophie Devine was born in Wellington, New Zealand in 1989.

Devine made her debut for New Zealand cricket in a Twenty20 match against Australia in October 2006 and, four days later, played in her first ODI for New Zealand against the same opposition.

Since her international debuts, she has played, up to New Zealand's tour to India at the end of June 2015, 63 ODIs for New Zealand and 47 Twenty20 matches; in her 63 ODIs, she has scored 1,080 runs at an average of 23.47 with her highest score of 145 being her only century to date; with her medium pace bowling, she has picked up 43 wickets at 39.93 apiece, with best figures of three for 38. In her 47 Twenty20 international matches, she has scored 862 runs at an average of 22.68 with a top score of 59 and taken 40 wickets at an average of 17.07, with best figures of three for 9.

Devine has also represented New Zealand at hockey; however, having signed a contract with New Zealand cricket, her opportunities to continue playing international hockey are more limited and she was overlooked by the selectors for the Commonwealth Games in 2014.

37. George Dickinson (1903-1978), *New Zealand rugby player and cricketer*

George Dickinson was born in 1903 in Dunedin, New Zealand.

After playing in the Otago Boys' High School for four years from 1918 until 1921, Dickinson made his first-class debut at rugby in 1922 at the age of 19 when picked to play for South Island. In the same year, before having played for his Province Otago, he was selected to play for New Zealand on a tour to Australia, where he played in four matches for New Zealand, three against New South Wales and one against a New South Wales B team. Later in the same year, he turned out again for New Zealand in a home fixture against a New Zealand Maori XV. In his five matches representing New Zealand, three of which were won and two lost, Dickinson played at both fly-half and centre, scoring three tries.

He never played in a Test match for New Zealand at rugby and retired from the game in 1924 at the age of 21, having played 12 times for Otago between 1922 and 1924.

As well as being a rugby player, Dickinson was also a fast bowler and played his first game of cricket for Otago in the 1921/22 season. He continued to play for Otago until the 1937/38 season and played one game for Wellington in the 1943/44 season. He was first selected to play cricket for New Zealand against Victoria in 1925, making him the first to represent New Zealand at both rugby and cricket; he played two more games for New Zealand, one a second game against Victoria in 1925 and the other a game against Australia in 1928, before he played his first Test match which was against the touring England side in 1929/30 – New Zealand had not been granted Test status when he played against Australia in 1928. Dickinson played in two Tests against England and his third and final Test was two years later against South Africa. In his three Tests, he scored 31 runs at an average of 6.20 and took eight wickets at an average of 30.62. He fared better in his 39 first-class games – he scored 1,103 runs, including one century, at an average of 18.75 and took 150 wickets at an average of 26.96, including best figures of seven for 90 against Wellington.

After retiring from cricket, Dickinson continued his career as a commercial traveller, something which had impacted on his career in sport. He died at the age of 75, in 1978.

38. Lottie Dod (1871-1960), *English tennis player, golfer, archer and hockey player*

Charlotte "Lottie" Dod was born in Bebington, Merseyside in 1871.

In 1887, she entered Wimbledon, beating the defending champion Blanche Bingley in the challenge round and thereby became, at the age of 15 years and 285 days, the youngest woman ever to have won the Ladies Championships. She successfully defended her title in the following two years, both Challenge Round finals being against Blanche Bingley. Dod did not defend her title in 1890 or compete in 1891 but regained the title in 1892 and 1893, winning both finals, with Blanche Bingley losing to her for the fourth and fifth time in finals. Dod did not compete again at Wimbledon, leaving her with a record not only of being the youngest ever winner but also of never losing at Wimbledon in the five times she took part. In her entire tennis career, she only ever lost five matches and only once after the age of 15.

Between 1895 and 1897, Dod took an interest in Winter sports and, as well as tobogganing the Cresta Run at St Moritz and mountaineering with one of her brothers during this period, she became the second woman ever to pass the St Moritz Men's Skating Test.

By 1897, Dod had taken up hockey and, in 1899, was selected to play for England against Ireland, a match won 3-1 by England. She played in her second, and last, hockey international in 1900 in a return match against Ireland, scoring both goals in a 2-1 victory. A bout of sciatica and mourning following her mother's death put a premature end to her international hockey career.

Dod had started playing golf at much the same time as she first played at Wimbledon and, by 1894, had entered the British Amateur Championships. In 1898 and 1900, she reached the semi-finals of these Championships. After 1900, she did not compete in the Championships again until 1904, when she won a close final against the 1899 and 1902 champion, May Hezlet. In winning the British Women's Amateur Golf Championship, she became the only person to have won the tennis championships at Wimbledon and the British Amateur Golf Championships.

Later in 1904, Dod took part in the American Amateur Golf Championships but did not progress beyond the first round. The following year, she represented Britain in a match against America and England in matches against Ireland and Wales, which were staged before the 1905 Amateur Championships, which she competed in, losing in the fourth round.

1905 also saw Dod move south, to Newbury in Berkshire, where she joined the Welford Park Archery Club. By finishing 5th in the Grand National Archery meetings in 1906, 1907 and 1908, she earned herself a place in the British Olympic Archery team at the 1908 Olympics. After the first day, she was in the lead but, after being overtaken on the second day by her compatriot Queenie Newall, had to settle for the silver medal – one of her brothers, Willy, had also been selected and went one better when winning the gold medal in the men's event.

Dod's sporting career came to an end when the Welford Park Archery Club disbanded in 1911. She served as a nurse during the First World War and eventually died peacefully, as a spinster, in a nursing home in 1960, at the age of 88. Later, she was named by the Guinness Book of Records as one of the two most versatile sportswomen of all time, along with Babe Zaharias (see Chapter 172).

39. Martin Donnelly (1917-1999), *New Zealand cricketer and English rugby player*

Martin Donnelly was born in 1917 in Ngaruawahia in New Zealand.

After just one first-class game of cricket, Donnelly was selected as a member of the New Zealand team to tour England in 1937 and played in all three Tests on the tour. He continued playing for Wellington until 1941 but, after the Second World War, in which he served as a tank commander in North Africa and Italy, he went to Oxford University. In 1946, he scored a century in the Varsity Match and a year later captained the Oxford team; as a result of his performances in 1947 at Oxford, he was one of Wisden's cricketers of the year, in 1948. After graduating, Donnelly played cricket for Warwickshire in 1948 and 1950; in between his years at Warwickshire, he played for New Zealand on their tour to England, playing in all four Tests.

He retired from playing Test cricket after the 1949 tour, having only played in seven Tests, all of which were in England and in which he scored 582 runs at an average of 52.90. The highlight of his Test career was the 206 he scored against England at Lord's in 1949.

Although Donnelly only played 13 first-class games of cricket in his native New Zealand, he played in a total of 131 first-class games, most of which were for Oxford University and Warwickshire. His last match for Warwickshire was in 1950 and, after that, he only played one more game of first-class cricket, for the New Zealand Governor-General's XI against the MCC in 1961. In all first-class matches, he scored 9,250 runs at an average of 47.43, including 23 centuries and a highest score of 208 not out; he also took 43 wickets at an average of 39.13.

Whilst at Oxford, Donnelly also played rugby for the University team at fly-half and earned himself one cap, playing centre for England in 1947 in England's only defeat in the Five Nations that season, a 22-0 loss to Ireland.

After retiring from Test cricket, Donnelly went into business; his relatively brief cricket career was long enough though for C. B. Fry (see Chapter 50) to describe him being as good a left-hander as any he had seen. Dickinson died at the age of 82, in 1999.

40. J. W. H. T. Douglas (1882-1930), *English Olympian boxer, cricketer and footballer*

John William Henry Taylor Douglas, also known as Johnny Douglas and JWHT Douglas, was born in Stoke Newington, London in 1882.

Douglas won the ABA Middleweight title at boxing in 1905. Three years later, he was competing in the Olympics and after winning three bouts on the same day, took the gold medal in the Middleweight division. His performance in his final bout was described by The Times as "one of the most brilliant exhibitions of skilful boxing, allied to tremendous hitting, ever seen", although supporters of the silver medallist Snowy Baker (see Chapter 7) later claimed, without justification, that Douglas had only won because his father was the sole judge and referee.

Before winning his ABA title, Douglas had already represented Essex at cricket, first playing for them in 1902. He did not play for Essex in 1903, choosing instead to play for London County but returned to Essex in 1904 and stayed with them until his retirement in 1928, captaining them from 1911. He was first selected to play for England in 1911 and played a total of 23 Tests, in 18 of which he was captain. His last Test was in 1924, by which time he had scored a total of 962 runs, including a top score of 119 (his only century) at an average of 29.15 and taken, with his fast-medium pace, 45 wickets at an average of 33.02, with a best bowling analysis of five for 46. In all first-class cricket, he played in a total of 651 matches, scoring 24,531 runs at an average of 27.90 and taking 1,893 wickets at an average of 23.32. His best bowling analysis of nine for 46 came in the same match as his best score of 210 not out, one of 26 centuries scored by him.

Douglas also occasionally turned out at football for the one of the leading amateur clubs, Corinthian Casuals. Over the period from 1910 to 1923, he played 15 times for them and was good enough to play in one amateur game for England (although, due to the records being lost, there is no record of when it was or who the opposition was).

Douglas died in 1930 at the age of 48 when a boat on which he was travelling with his father collided with another boat in foggy conditions off the coast of Denmark – the collision happened when the captains of the two boats, who were brothers, were trying to exchange Christmas greetings. Douglas is believed to have been trying to save his father when he drowned.

41. Ted Drake (1912-1994), *English footballer and cricketer*

Ted Drake was born in Southampton in 1912.

Drake played cricket for Hampshire in 16 first-class matches between 1931 and 1936; in his 16 matches, he scored 219 runs, averaging 8.11 and with a top score of 45 and took four wickets at an average of 42.75.

Drake had more success as a footballer. He played 74 games for Southampton between 1931 and 1934, scoring 48 goals for them before moving to Arsenal for a fee of £6,500. Over the next 10 seasons, Drake made 184 appearances for Arsenal, scoring 139 goals. With Arsenal, Drake played in two championship winning teams (1934/35 and 1937/38) and, in 1936, won the F. A. Cup, scoring the only goal in the final against Sheffield United. His goal-scoring feats at Arsenal include scoring all seven goals in a 7-1 victory at Aston Villa – an eighth goal was disallowed but seven goals in one match is still the highest in the top division of English football.

Drake's performances at Arsenal led to international recognition; Drake played five times for England between 1934 and 1938, scoring six goals for them, including a hat-trick in a 6-2 win over Hungary in 1936.

After the War, Drake retired as a player and went into football management. He spent one season with Hendon Town before spending five seasons with Reading Town. He then managed Chelsea for nine years, taking them to their first league championship title in the 1954/55 season.

After managing Chelsea, he was appointed reserve team manager at Fulham before becoming one of their directors.

Drake died in 1994 at the age of 82.

42. Andy Ducat (1886-1942), *English cricketer and footballer*

Andy Ducat was born in Brixton in 1886.

Ducat played non-league football for Southend United before joining Arsenal in 1905. During his seven years with Arsenal, he played in 188 matches for them, scoring 22 goals; his success at Arsenal brought him national recognition and, in 1910, he played three games for England. His first international was a 1-1 draw with Ireland but, in his second game, he scored the only goal in a 1-0 win over Wales; his third match saw England lose 2-0 to Scotland.

In 1912, Ducat joined Aston Villa, but a broken leg in his first season and the First World War disrupted his career there; his injury prevented him playing in the 1913 F. A. Cup Final. However, in 1920, he captained Aston Villa to F. A. Cup success and recaptured his place in the England team 10 years after his last international, playing in all three of England's Home Championship fixtures.

In 1921, Ducat joined Fulham for whom he played for three seasons before becoming their manager; two years later, he was sacked as their manager.

Ducat's first-class cricket career with Surrey started in 1906 and, by the time he retired in 1931, he had played 429 games of first-class cricket, including one Test for England, the third Test against the touring Australians in 1921. In all his first-class matches, Ducat scored 23,373 runs at an average of 38.31, with 52 centuries to his name and a highest score of 306 not out; his rarely-used bowling brought him 21 wickets at a cost of 43 runs per wicket and best bowling figures of three for 12. He was less successful in his only Test, scoring just 3 and 2 in his two innings; in the first innings, he was out in two ways – he was caught at slip but, when hitting the ball, his bat broke and a splinter dislodged a bail, thereby being out "hit wicket" as well; the scorecard records his dismissal as caught.

After retiring from cricket in 1931, Ducat took up the position of cricket coach at Eton College and also worked as a sports reporter. Whilst playing in a match at Lord's in 1942 between two Home Guard teams, Ducat had a suspected heart attack and died, at the age of 56; against his name, the scoreboard read "Not Out Dead" and he remains the only cricketer to have died whilst playing in a match at Lord's.

43. Eddie Eagen (1897-1967), *American Olympic boxer and bobsleigher*

Eddie Eagen was born in 1897 in Denver, Colorado.

In 1919, Eagen won America's Amateur Athletic Union title for boxing. A year later, he was competing at the Olympics in Antwerp and took the gold medal for the light heavyweight division. After attending Yale University and Harvard Law School, Eagen won a Rhodes Scholarship to Oxford in 1922 and, whilst at Oxford, won the British Amateur heavyweight title. In 1924, he competed again in the Olympics in the heavyweight division but lost to Britain's Arthur Clifton in the first round; having injured his hands against Eagen, Clifton withdrew before his second round bout.

Eagen returned to compete in the Olympics eight years later, at the Winter Olympics in Lake Placid, where he teamed up with Billy Fiske to win the gold in the bobsleigh event. Eagen's win in the bobsleigh event made him the only man to have won a gold medal at both the Summer Olympics and Winter Olympics in different events.

After his sporting days were over, Eagen worked as a lawyer. He died in 1967 at the age of 70.

Author's note: Sweden's Gillis Grafstrom won gold medals at both the 1920 Summer Olympics and the Winter Olympics in 1924 and 1928, his wins all being for figure skating, which had been an event at the Summer Olympics in 1920 and an event at the Winter Olympics in 1924 and 1928.

44. Kim Elgie (1933-   ), *South African cricketer and Scottish rugby player*

Michael Kelsey "Kim" Elgie was born in Durban, South Africa in 1933.

Whilst attending St Andrews University in the 1950s, Elgie was selected to play rugby for Scotland at centre. His first match for Scotland was against the touring All Black team in February 1954. He then played for Scotland in their remaining three Five Nations Championships in 1954 and in all four of their Five Nations Championship matches in 1955. Although they only narrowly lost 0-3 in Elgie's first match against the All Blacks, Scotland picked up the Wooden Spoon in 1954, losing all four of their Five Nations matches, although Elgie did manage to score a try against England in Scotland's 3-13 defeat. The 1955 Five Nations Championships saw Elgie record his only two wins in international rugby, one against Wales (a game in which Elgie kicked a conversion and a penalty) and the other against Ireland (in which he kicked two penalties).

On returning to South Africa, Elgie played cricket for Natal from 1957 until 1962, batting right-handed and bowling slow left-arm orthodox. He was selected to play in three Tests for South Africa in the five Test series against the visiting New Zealand team. In his six innings in the three Tests, Elgie only scored 75 runs at an average of 12.50, with a highest score of 56. He did not take a wicket in his 11 overs, which only cost 18 runs. He played a total of 32 first-class games of cricket, scoring 1,834 runs at an average of 36.67 and taking 10 wickets at an average of 40.50. His runs included three centuries and his highest score of 162 not out came in one of cricket's more extraordinary matches, the one between Natal and Border in 1959. Elgie was batting at number 3 for Natal and came to the crease without a run on the board; he managed to score 11 before being fourth man out, Natal eventually scrambling to 90 all out. In reply, in their first innings, Border managed only 16 runs in total, equalling the 10th lowest score in first-class cricket. Second time round, Natal fared much better, declaring on 294 for 8, with Elgie on 162 not out and setting Border a target of 369 to win; Border however fared only marginally better in their second innings, scoring a total of 18 – their total of 34 for both innings remains the lowest in first-class cricket; a match in which Elgie scored his highest innings of 162 not out had seen 34 wickets taken of batsmen who could muster no more than 49 runs between them.

After university, Elgie trained as an optometrist.

45. Russell Endean (1924-2003), *South African cricketer and hockey player*

William Russell Endean was born in Johannesburg in 1924.

After the Second World War, in which he served in Egypt and Italy, Endean played cricket for Transvaal, making his debut in 1946 and, in 1951, was chosen to tour England with the South African team as a wicketkeeper/batsman. He only played in one Test on this tour, the fifth and final Test at the Oval; whilst keeping wicket during this match, umpire Frank Chester gave Len Hutton out for obstructing the field when Hutton, who thought the ball running off his arm would drop on to the stumps, instinctively flicked his bat and thereby, in Chester's view, impeded Endean from catching the ball – this is the only case of a batsman being dismissed for obstructing the field in a Test match.

Over the period from 1951 to 1957, Endean played a total of 28 Tests, during which he scored 1,650 runs at an average of 33.95, with three centuries and a top score of 162 not out to his name; he only kept wicket in his first Test, but, in addition to the three catches he took as wicketkeeper in his first Test, he took another 38 catches as a fielder in his other 27 Tests.

As well as being involved in the only Test dismissal for obstructing the ball, Endean was also the first Test cricketer to be dismissed for handling the ball; in the second Test of England's tour to South Africa in 1956/57, Endean was given out for handling the ball when he tried to stop the ball, which he had top-edged, from hitting the stumps; Endean said afterwards that he had thought of heading the ball away, which would have saved his wicket, but he considered that too theatrical.

Endean played a total of 158 games of first-class cricket. He scored a total of 7,757 runs at an average of 37.83, hitting 15 centuries and a top score of 247 – one of his centuries was the 235 he scored against Orange Free State in 1954, when he made the highest score in a pre-lunch session, 197 not out.

Prior to playing cricket for South Africa, Endean had played for South Africa at hockey.

After playing his last game of cricket for Transvaal in 1961, Endean settled in England working as an accountant. He died in England in 2003 at the age of 79.

46. John Evans (1889-1961), *English cricketer and golfer*

Alfred John Evans was born in Newtown, Hampshire, in 1889.

Over a first-class cricket career spanning 20 years from 1908, Evans only played in 90 games, scoring 3,499 runs at an average of 24.64, with six centuries and a top score of 143; he also took 110 wickets at an average of 27.83 with best bowling figures of seven for 50.

Following a score of 69 not out for the MCC against the touring Australians, he was selected to play in the second Test against them in 1921 but, after scores of 4 and 14, was not selected to play again for England.

Evans's cricket career was interrupted by the First World War, in which he served as a pilot in the Royal Flying Corps before being captured and held as a prisoner-of-war until his escape; he wrote about his experience as a prisoner-of-war and his exploits escaping in The Escaping Club.

As well as being a Test cricketer, Evans was also a golfer and took part in the 1928 British Open Championships as an amateur. He played in all four rounds and, although he finished 27 shots behind the winner Walter Hagen, he came sixth amongst the amateurs.

Evans died in 1961 at the age of 71.

47. Steven Ferguson (1980-   ), *New Zealand swimmer, canoeist and lifesaver*

Steven Ferguson was born in Auckland in 1980.

Ferguson represented New Zealand in swimming events at the 1998 Commonwealth Games and at the 2000 Olympics in Sydney, where he failed to progress beyond the qualifying heats in the 100 metres and 200 metres breaststroke.

Ferguson also represented New Zealand at the 2004, 2008 and 2012 Olympics in the canoeing events, recording his best place, 5th, at the 2008 Games in the K-2 1,000 metres with Mike Walker.

Ferguson is also a surf lifesaver and represented New Zealand at the World Lifesaving Championships in 2004 and 2006.

Ferguson's father, Ian, won four gold medals in canoeing events at the Olympics (three in 1984 and one in 1988) and two gold medals at the World Championships (in 1985 and 1987).

48. Tip Foster (1878-1914), *English cricketer and footballer*

Reginald Erskine "Tip" Foster was born in Malvern in 1878.

After leaving school, Foster went to Oxford University, which he represented at rackets, golf, cricket and football. He played cricket for the University side from 1897 to 1900 and in his last year, scored 171 in the Varsity Match, which was, at the time, the highest score in this fixture. In all his matches for Oxford that year, he scored a total of 930 runs at an average of 77.50, still a record for University cricket.

1900 also saw him selected for the annual Gentleman v. Players fixture; in this match, he became the first batsman to score centuries in both innings.

Whilst at Oxford, Foster also played for Worcestershire - Tip was one of seven brothers, all of whom played cricket for Worcestershire. In the match against Hampshire in 1899, he and one of his brothers both scored two centuries, a feat which has not been repeated in county cricket by any brothers since.

Foster's performances in 1900 resulted in him being nominated as one of Wisden's Cricketers of the Year in 1901 and, in 1903, he played in his first Test, against Australia in Sydney. On his debut, he scored 287, which was, until 1930, the highest score in Test cricket and remains the highest score by a debutant.

In 1907, Foster was captain of the England team against the visiting South Africans, making him the first and only man to have captained England at both football and cricket. After the 1907 series against South Africa, he only played two more games of first-class cricket.

In total, Foster played in eight Test matches for England. He scored a total of 602 runs at an average of 46.30, his only century being his 287 on debut. In first-class cricket, he played in 139 matches, scoring 9,076 runs, including 22 centuries, at an average of 41.82 and took 25 wickets at an average of 46.12.

As well as playing football for Oxford University, Foster also played for the Corinthians and was selected to play for England in 1900. He played in five matches for England between 1900 and 1902, winning two of them and drawing the other three; in his second international, against Ireland in 1901, a game in which C. B. Fry (see Chapter 50) made his only appearance for England at football, Foster scored two goals in a 3-0 victory. Foster scored his third and final goal for England in their 6-0 win over Wales in 1901 and, in his fifth and final game, he captained the England team. Foster also played football for the England amateur team and, in the first ever game against Germany, scored six goals in a 12-0 win.

In 1913, Foster was diagnosed with diabetes and died a year later at the age of 36.

49. Heinz Frei (1958-   ), *Swiss Paralympian athlete, skier and cyclist*

Heinz Frei was born in Switzerland in 1958.

Frei has represented Switzerland in both the Summer Paralympic Games and the Winter Paralympic Games. He first competed in the Summer Paralympic Games in athletics events in 1984 and appeared again later that year at the Winter Paralympic Games, competing in the cross-country skiing events. He continued to represent his country in the Summer Games up until 2008 and at the Winter Games until 2006.

As well as taking part in the athletics events at the Summer Games, Frei has also taken part in the cycling events and, at the Winter Games, has taken part in skiing events and the biathlon. His medals tally is 31, with 14 gold medals, six silver medals and 11 bronze medals to his name; of his gold medals, 11 were won in athletics events, one in cycling and two in cross-country skiing - only the American swimmer Trisha Zom has won more medals than Frei at the Paralympic Games.

As well as being a successful Paralympian, Frei has also won numerous wheelchair marathons and half-marathons. He has held the world record at both distances and his wins include the London wheelchair marathon in 1995, 1998 and 1999, the Berlin wheelchair marathon in 1997 and 2013 and the Boston wheelchair marathon in 1994 and 1996.

50. C. B. Fry (1872-1956), *English cricketer, athlete, footballer and rugby player*

Charles Burgess Fry was born in Croydon in 1872.

Fry went up to Oxford University in 1891 where he studied classics for four years. During his four years at University, he played for and captained the cricket and football teams and was president of the athletics club; an injury denied him a blue at rugby as well.

Before he had left school Fry had played football in the F. A. Cup at the age of 16 for The Casuals, a leading amateur club. Whilst at University and for six years after graduating, he also played football for the Corinthians, another leading amateur club but, to improve his chances of selection at an international level, he joined Southampton FC in 1901. Whilst at Southampton, he was picked to play for England at full-back in their match against Ireland, a match which resulted in a 3-0 win for England.

During the 1901/02 season, Fry played in all Southampton's games in the F. A. Cup that year, a run that saw them lose in the final to Sheffield United after a replay. Overall, Fry played 25 games for Southampton before moving to Portsmouth, for whom he made three appearances before retiring through injury.

Fry's athletics career did not continue after his University years. He won his blue in all four years he was at Oxford, taking part in the long jump in all four years, the high jump in 1892 and the 100 yards in 1893 and 1894. In 1892, he broke the British record for the long jump and a year later equalled the world record for the long jump, a record which lasted 18 months.

Although he failed to win a blue at rugby because of injury, Fry was good enough to play for Blackheath on 10 occasions and was selected to play in three matches for the Barbarians; he was the first reserve for the South team in their match against the North, a fixture very much seen as an England trial.

Cricket is however the sport for which Fry is probably best remembered. He first represented Surrey in 1891 in a game which was not a first-class match. He played for Oxford University from 1892 to 1895, for Sussex from 1894 to 1908 and for Hampshire from 1909 to 1921. During his first-class career, he scored 30,886 runs, including 94 centuries and a top score of 258 not out, at an average of 50.22; his bowling accounted for 166 wickets at an average of 29.34 – on two occasions, he took ten wickets in a match. He headed the national batting averages in six years between 1901 and 1912 and, in 1901, hit six centuries in consecutive innings, a feat which has only been matched twice, once by the great Don Bradman and once by the great all-rounder Mike Proctor.

Fry was first selected to play cricket for England on the 1895/96 tour to South Africa. He continued to play for England until 1912, when he captained them in three Tests against Australia (a series England won 1-0 with two matches drawn) and three against South Africa (a series won 3-0 by England). In his 26 Test matches, he scored 1,223 runs, including two centuries and a top score of 144, at an average of 32.18.

After graduating, Fry taught for two years before turning his hand to journalism. In the 1920s, he tried his luck in politics, standing as the Liberal candidate for Brighton in the 1922 General Election, for Banbury in the 1923 General Election and for Oxford in a by-election in 1924, in each case, losing out in closely fought seats. Another political position discussed with him at this time was the vacant throne of Albania, which Fry claimed was offered to him through his connection at The League of Nations, at which his Sussex teammate Ranjitsinhji was a representative for India.

Fry died in 1956 at the age of 84. In his obituary in Wisden 1957, the English cricket writer Neville Cardus wrote of him that he "belonged – and it was his glory - to an age not obsessed by specialism; he was one of the last of the English tradition of the amateur, the connoisseur and, in the most delightful sense of the word, the dilettante". His gravestone, near Repton where he was at school, is inscribed "1872 CB Fry 1956 – cricketer, scholar, athlete, author – the Ultimate All-rounder". His all-round abilities were not limited though to just athletics, cricket, football and rugby; he also excelled at fishing, golf, skating, skiing, rowing and tennis and, to many, he is considered not only the greatest all-round sportsman of his time but also of all time.

51. Divina Galica (1944-   ), *English skier and motor racer*

Divina Galica was born in Hertfordshire in 1944.

Galica was first selected as a member of the British Women's Olympics Ski Team in 1964 and, at the 1968 and 1972 Winter Olympics, captained the Ski Team. At all three Winter Games, she participated in the downhill, the giant slalom and the slalom. At the 1964 Winter Games, she did not qualify for the slalom event but came 30th in the downhill and 23rd in the giant slalom. Four years later, her performances in the downhill, in which she came 32nd and the slalom, which she did not finish, were similar to her performances in 1964 but her performance in the giant slalom, in coming 8th, had significantly improved. At the 1972 Winter Games, she recorded her best results in all three events, coming 26th in the downhill, 15th in the slalom and 7th in the giant slalom.

Although she recorded her best Olympic results in 1972, Galica's best performances in the World Cup were in 1968; after securing two podium finishes when coming 3rd in the downhill events at Chamonix and Badgastein, she finished 12th overall that season.

Galica made her fourth Winter Olympic appearance in 1972 when she took part in the speed skiing event, a demonstration sport at these Games. As a speed skier, she held the British record with a speed of 125 mph.

Following the 1972 Winter Games, Galica took up motor racing after accepting an invitation to take part in a celebrity auto race. By 1976, she had entered the British Grand Prix in a Surtees car, making her only the third women to have raced in a Grand Prix event but, in a car numbered 13, the first time for 13 years a car had been raced with this number, her luck ran out and she failed to qualify. Two years later, she was offered the opportunity to race again in Formula 1 in a Hesketh car; after failing to qualify for the first two races of the year, in Argentina and Brazil, she returned to the British Formula 1 Series and a year later was racing in the European Formula 2 races.

Galica was awarded the MBE after the 1972 Winter Olympics.

52. Leslie Gay (1871-1949), *English cricketer, footballer and golfer*

Leslie Gay was born in Brighton in 1871.

Gay was the wicketkeeper for Cambridge University in the Varsity match against Oxford University in 1892 and 1893 and, after playing four games for Somerset in 1894, was picked for the England team visiting Australia in 1894/95. The only Test he played in was the first one, which England won by 10 runs despite being 261 runs behind after the first innings. Gay's contribution was scores of 33 and 4 with the bat, three catches and a stumping.

After returning to England, Gay gave up cricket for five years, before appearing eight times for Hampshire in 1900. When he retired finally, he had played 46 games of first-class cricket, scoring a total of 1,005 runs, with a top score of 60 not out, at an average of 15.46, taken 70 catches and made 20 stumpings.

As well as playing cricket for Cambridge, Gay also played in goal in the 1892 Varsity football match. He also played football for the Old Brightonians and the Corinthians and, whilst playing for these amateur clubs, was selected to play for England. His first international appearance was against Scotland in 1893, a match won by England 5-2. A year later he was selected to play against Scotland again, a match which was drawn 2-2 and in the fixture against Wales, which England won 5-1. In 1900, he joined Southampton FC but, as Southampton's goalkeeper at the time was also the England goalkeeper, Gay never got a game in the Southampton first team.

In the First World War, Gay served as a major. Later in life, Gay took up golf, at which he represented Devon, the county in which he died in 1949 at the age of 78.

53. M. J. Gopalan (1909-2003), *Indian cricketer and hockey player*

Morappakam Josyam Gopalan was born near Madras and his birth was recorded as being in 1909 although he and his family claimed it had been three years earlier.

Gopalan made his debut in first-class cricket in 1927 and, by the time he retired in 1950, he had played 78 games of first-class cricket, including one Test match. His one Test, the second Test against England in 1934, was a drawn match in which he scored 11 not out and 7 and took one wicket for 39 runs.

In all first-class games, he scored 2,916 runs at an average of 24.92, with one century, a score of 101 not out, to his name and took 194 wickets at an average of 24.20.

Gopalan's cricket achievements include captaining Madras and South India and, in 1930, dismissing Sir Jack Hobbs twice in a match when he was playing for the Vizianagram XI against Madras. Gopalan also bowled the first ever ball in the Ranji Trophy when it was first competed for back in 1934.

Gopalan also played hockey for Madras and India. He played centre-half and was selected to tour Ceylon, Australia and New Zealand in 1935;

in their one match against Australia, India won 12-1 and, against New Zealand, they won all three matches with scores of 4-2, 4-3 and 7-1; overall, India played 48 matches on the tour, winning them all scoring 584 goals in the process and with Gopalan playing in 39 of them. A year later, Gopalan was selected to play for India at hockey at the Berlin Olympics as well as for the Indian cricket team touring England. As he was unable to do both, instead of choosing to play at the Olympics, where India were favourites to win the gold, he opted to tour with the cricketers – in hindsight, this proved to be an unwise decision as he was not picked to play in any of the three Tests, whilst the hockey players, under the captaincy of Dhyan Chand, considered by many to have been the greatest hockey player of all time, duly picked up the gold medal.

After retiring from cricket, Gopalan became a selector and, to commemorate his 25 years as a cricketer and hockey player, an annual cricket fixture between Madras and Ceylon was arranged, playing for the Gopalan Trophy; this first fixture took place in 1953 and continued until Sri Lanka was granted Test status in 1983.

Gopalan died in 2003, having been, immediately prior to his death, the oldest surviving Test cricketer.

54. Andy Goram (1964-   ), *Scottish footballer and cricketer*

Andy Goram was born in Bury, Lancashire in 1964.

Goram joined Oldham Athletic in 1981 and made 195 league appearances in goal for them, before he was transferred north of the border for £325,000 to the club his father had played for, Hibernian. Whilst at Oldham, he was named in the England Under-21 squad but, as he never played for them, remained eligible to play for Scotland; he was also included, at the end of the 1986/87 season, in the PFA's Team of the Year for the English second division.

Goram spent four seasons with Hibs, making 138 league appearances for them, before moving to Rangers for a fee of £1,000,000; whilst at Hibs,

Goram scored the only goal of his career, a kick out from his own penalty area in the last game of the 1987/88 season, against Morton.

In Goram's first season with Rangers, they won the Scottish Cup and the Scottish Premier League and, in his second year, they did even better, adding the Scottish League Cup to the Scottish Cup and the Premier League. His performances in his second year at Rangers earned him player of the year awards from both the Scottish Football Writers and the Scottish Professional Footballers Association.

Goram left Rangers at the end of the 1987/88 season, having made 184 league appearances for them and having won six Premier Division titles, three Scottish Cups and two Scottish League Cups with them. In 2001, he was voted in a poll by Rangers' fans as the club's best goalkeeper of all time.

After one game for Notts County and seven games for Sheffield United, Goram joined Motherwell where he stayed for three seasons. After Motherwell, Goram continued playing until the end of the 2003/04 season, playing a few games for a number of different clubs.

Goram's international career with Scotland began whilst he was still at Oldham but it was not until after the 1990 World Cup that he became Scotland's first choice goalkeeper. Goram continued playing for Scotland until 1998 but his international career came to an end when he was not selected for the 1998 World Cup; by then, Goram had played 43 games for Scotland.

Goram was also a cricketer who batted left-handed and bowled right-arm medium pace; he played four times for Scotland, twice in their first-class matches against Ireland and twice in the NatWest Trophy; in his two games against Ireland, he scored 48 runs at an average of 16 and took two wickets for 39.

Since retiring from playing football, Goram has been goalkeeping coach for a number of Scottish clubs.

Goram remains the only man to have represented Scotland at football and in first-class cricket matches.

55. W. G. Grace (1848-1915), *English cricketer, athlete and bowls player*

William Gilbert Grace, better known as Dr W. G. Grace, was born in Bristol in 1848.

He was brought up at a time when the popularity of cricket was spreading, particularly amongst the middle class to which he and his family belonged. By the age of 15, he had represented West Gloucestershire in a match against an All England XI and a year later made his first century, for South Wales CC against The Gentlemen of Sussex.

In 1871, Grace became the first man to score 2,000 runs in a season and two years later, the first man to score 2,000 runs and take 100 wickets in a season, a feat he repeated for the next five seasons and twice in the 1880s.

In 1876, he scored what was then the highest score in first-class cricket, an innings of 344, playing for the Gentlemen of the MCC against Kent and, within a week, had scored 177 for Gloucestershire against Nottinghamshire and another triple century, this time 318 not out, against Yorkshire.

In 1895, at the age of 46, he became the first man to score 1,000 runs in May and, in 1895, was the first cricketer to score 100 centuries.

Grace's first-class cricket career lasted from 1865 until 1908; during this time, he played for 28 different first-class teams, but the majority of his matches were for Gloucestershire for whom he played from 1870 until 1899. Not only was Grace the leading run-scorer over this period, he was also the leading wicket-taker. When he retired, he had scored 54,896 runs (the fifth highest in first-class cricket) at an average of 39.55 and taken 2,876 wickets (the sixth highest in first-class cricket) at an average of 17.92 runs per wicket; he was also a fine fielder, taking a total of 887 catches – he also had a strong throwing arm and, at an athletics event, once threw a cricket ball 122 yards. His total of 126 centuries is the 11th most and on 66 occasions, he took 10 wickets or more in a match.

Grace did not enjoy the same success as a Test cricketer as he had in his other first-class matches. In his 22 Tests, between 1880 and 1899, he made just 1,098 runs, at an average of 32.29 and only scored two centuries and took just nine wickets, at an average of 26.22 – the first of his Test centuries, a score of 152, was on his debut against Australia, a match in which his brothers E. M. and George also played for England.

By the time Grace retired from cricket, his shape was such that it is difficult to imagine that, in his youth, he had been a champion athlete; in 1866, he won the 440 yards hurdles title at the National Olympic Games at Crystal Palace. He also played football for the leading amateur team The Wanderers, but not in any of their teams that won the F. A. Cup six times in the 1870s.

Before he had retired from cricket, Grace had taken up bowls. He captained England in their first ever international bowls match, against Scotland in 1903 and continued to captain the England team until 1908; and, after retiring from cricket, he took up curling and golf.

Grace's sporting achievements did not prevent Grace continuing with his medical studies and, in 1879, he qualified as a doctor in 1879, allowing him to carry on his own private practice, employing locums during the cricket season.

Grace's record and reputation as a cricketer, not least his reputation for gamesmanship, have allowed his other sporting achievements to be overlooked, such was his contribution to popularising the game in the second half of the 19th century. C. R. L. James credited Grace with transforming the game of cricket into a national institution and 60 years after Grace's death from a heart attack in 1915, David Frith wrote of Grace being "the most famous cricketer of them all" and the one who "elevated the game in public esteem".

56. Sam Guillen (1924-2013), *West Indian cricketer, cyclist and footballer*

Simpson Clairmonte Guillen, better known as Sam Guillen, was born in Trinidad in 1924.

In 1951, Guillen was chosen to tour Australia and New Zealand with the West Indies cricket team and made his debut in the third Test against Australia. On the tour, he played in three Tests against Australia and two against New Zealand, scoring 104 runs at an average of 26 and with a top score of 54; as wicketkeeper, he also took nine catches and made two stumpings.

At the end of the tour, Guillen decided to stay on in New Zealand. At first, Guillen turned down the opportunity to play cricket for Canterbury because he did not want a local cricketer to lose out at his expense but eventually he agreed to play for them and his performances led to him being selected, in 1956, as the New Zealand wicketkeeper for the team against the touring West Indians, making him the only West Indian Test cricketer to have played for two countries. He played in three of the four Tests, scoring 98 runs at an average of 16.33 and with a top score of 41; in addition to his four catches, he made one stumping against his former teammate Alf Valentine – his stumping of Valentine brought New Zealand their first win in Test cricket. Guillen retired from cricket immediately after this win.

Guillen's overall Test record was 202 runs at an average of an average of 20.2, 13 catches and three stumpings. In all first-class cricket, he played in 66 matches, scoring 2,672 runs at an average of 26.98, including three centuries and a top score of 197; he took 111 catches and made 34 stumpings and the 20 overs he bowled brought him one wicket for 49 runs.

Before emigrating to New Zealand, Guillen had been a champion cyclist back in Trinidad; in New Zealand, he took up football and, in 1954, played in goal for Western F.C. in New Zealand's provincial Chatham Cup Final, which they lost 1-0 to Onehunga.

Guillen was just one of a number of family members involved in cricket; his father Victor was a Test umpire and his brother also played for Trinidad and Tobago; and his grandson Logan van Beek played for The Netherlands in the 2014 Twenty20 World Cup. Guillen died in 2013 at the age of 88, whilst suffering from lung cancer.

57. Billy Gunn (1858-1921), *English cricketer and footballer*

Billy Gunn was born in Nottingham in 1858.

Gunn played his first game of first-class cricket for Nottinghamshire in 1880 and, by the time of his retirement in 1904, had played 521 first-class matches, having scored 25,691 runs, including 48 centuries and a top score of 273, at an average of 33.02. He was also recognised as one of the greatest fielders of his era, ending his career with 333 catches, whilst his slow underarm bowling brought him 76 wickets at an average of 23.68.

Gunn was selected to tour Australia with the England team in 1886/87 and made his debut early in 1887. He played in 11 Tests for England between 1887 and 1899, scoring 392 runs, including one century of 102 not out, at an average of 21.77.

Gunn also played football as an outside-left for Notts County and Nottingham Forest as an amateur. He was selected to play for England for two matches in 1884, the first against Scotland, which Scotland won 1-0 and the second against Wales, a match in which he scored one of the goals in a 4-0 victory. Gunn had also played for England in an unofficial match against Scotland in 1882 in which his long one-handed throw-ins led to the Football Association changing the law so that throw-ins could no longer be with only one hand.

After these appearances, Gunn played less football to allow him to play cricket more and devote time to the sports equipment company, Gunn and Moore, which he had founded in 1885 – bats manufactured by this company are still used by many of the world's best known cricketers.

Gunn died of cancer in 1921 at the age of 62.

58. Simon Halliday (1960-   ), *English rugby player and cricketer*

Simon Halliday was born in Haverfordwest, Wales in 1960.

Halliday played rugby at Oxford University from 1979 to 1981, playing in three Varsity matches against Cambridge University. After graduating, he joined Bath, where he played until 1990, winning five club knock-out competition titles with them before moving to Harlequins. Halliday retired from rugby in 1992 due to injuries.

In 1983, a week before he was due to make his debut for England, Halliday suffered a serious leg injury whilst playing for Somerset against Middlesex in the County Championship; after recovering, he was selected to play for England in 1986 and over the next six years played in 23 internationals, in which he scored two tries. 15 of his internationals were in the Five Nations and three in the 1991 Rugby World Cup, including in the final which England lost to Australia and in which Halliday played on the wing, despite playing for most of his career as a centre.

Whilst at Oxford, Halliday also played for the university cricket team in nine matches; five of his matches were in 1980, one being the Varsity match; his other four games were in 1982. He scored a total of 348 runs at an average of 29.00. His highlight was his first game in 1982, against a Kent team including the England bowlers Graham Dilley and Bob Woolmer; coming in to bat at 86 for 6, he and Ralph Cowan put on 129 for the seventh wicket and Halliday went on to make 117 not out; in reply, Kent's first four batsmen all scored centuries. Halliday was not able to maintain this form after the Kent match and, although he played three more matches for Oxford that season, he missed out on the Varsity match that year. After graduating, he continued to play cricket and, from 1981 to 1987, played in 38 Minor Counties Championship matches for Dorset.

Since his sporting days, Halliday has been a patron for the charities Cardiac Risk in the Young and Help for Heroes and has written an autobiography called City Centre, in which he tells not just of his life in sport but also of his time working in the City of London at the time of the collapse of Lehman Brothers.

59. Reginald Hands (1888-1918), *South African cricketer and English rugby player*

Reginald Hands was born in Cape Town in 1888.

Hands won a Rhodes Scholarship to Oxford University in 1910 and won a blue in rugby, following in the footsteps of his younger brother Philip, who had won a blue for rugby in 1908 and 1909; their younger brother Kenneth followed suit, winning his blue for rugby in 1912.

After a couple of trials playing for the South of England, Hands was picked to play rugby for England as a forward in 1910, in the Five Nations fixtures against France and Scotland, both won by England.

By 1913, Hands had returned to South Africa where he represented Western Province at cricket. In 1914, he was selected to play for South Africa against England in the last Test of their tour; also in the South African team was his brother Philip. England won the Test by 10 wickets and, in his two innings, Hands scored 0 and 7 – in both innings, Hands was stumped.

By the time the First World War had started, Hands had only played seven games of first-class cricket, in which he has scored 289 runs at an average of 28.90, with a top score of 79 not out; his six overs in first-class cricket brought no wickets and cost 22 runs.

Hands did not play any more first-class cricket after War had broken out in 1914 but his brother Philip went on to play seven Tests for South Africa up until 1924 and his other brother, Kenneth, also played first-class cricket for Western Province up until 1931.

As a result of injuries sustained on the Western Front whilst serving the South African Artillery, Hands died at the age of 29, in 1918.

60. Wally Hardinge (1886-1965), *English cricketer and footballer*

Harold Thomas William Hardinge, known as Wally, was born in Greenwich, Kent in 1886.

Hardinge played as a professional cricketer for Kent from 1902 until 1933, opening the batting right-handed and bowling slow left-arm. He was selected to play for England against Australia in one Test in 1925, a match in which he scored 25 and 5 but did not bowl. Australia won the match by 219 runs, aided by the absence of Jack Hobbs in both England's innings after suffering from appendicitis on the first day.

By the time he retired in 1933, Hardinge had played 623 games of first-class cricket. He scored a total of 33,519 runs at an average of 36.51 and took 371 wickets at an average 26.36, as well as taking 293 catches. He scored 1,000 runs or more in a season on 18 occasions and his runs included 75 centuries and a highest score of 263; his centuries included, in a match against Surrey in 1921, a double century and a century, making him the third cricketer to achieve this feat in the same match; his best bowling analysis was seven wickets for 64 runs but his most impressive bowling analysis was his six wickets for 9 runs in 11.5 overs in a match in 1929 against Warwickshire.

In his early years at Kent, Hardinge played amateur football before signing in 1905 as a professional with Newcastle United. He only made nine first team appearances for Newcastle before being sold to Sheffield United in 1907 for £350. He played in 154 matches for Sheffield United, scoring 46 goals before moving to Arsenal (then Woolwich Arsenal) in 1913. In 1910, whilst at Sheffield United, Hardinge was selected to play for England against Scotland in the Home Championships; a crowd of 106,205 at Hampden Park saw a 2-0 home win.

Hardinge's football career at Arsenal was interrupted by the First World War and he retired at the end of the 1919 season, having played 55 games for them (including their first game at Highbury), in which he scored 14 goals.

After retiring as a professional cricketer, Hardinge worked for John Wisden & Co Limited and briefly as a coach at Tottenham Hotspur.

He died in 1965 at the age of 79.

61. Heinrich Harrer (1912-2006), *Austrian skier, mountaineer and golfer*

Heinrich Harrer was born in Huttenberg in Austria, in 1912.

Whilst a student at Graz University, he was selected as a member of the Austrian alpine skiing team to take part in the 1936 Winter Olympics. However the banning of ski instructors from competing, because they were deemed to be professionals, led to the Austrian ski team boycotting the Games, thereby denying Harrer the opportunity to compete at the Games. A year later though Harrer won the downhill event at the World Student Championships.

Harrer was also very keen on mountain-climbing and, following his graduation in 1938, set off with his friend Fritz Kasparek to climb the North Face of the Eiger, a climb which had claimed a number of lives but never been conquered. During their ascent, they came across a German pair, Ludwig Vorg and Anderl Heckmair, also attempting to be the first to make the climb. The four teamed up and, after surviving an avalanche, became, on 24th July 1938, the first to climb the North Face of the Eiger.

Harrer was mountaineering in the Himalayas when the Second World War broke out and was placed in a detention camp in India. After a number of unsuccessful attempts, Harrer finally escaped in 1944 and headed with another escapee, Peter Aufschnaiter, for Tibet, which they finally reached in 1946. Harrer stayed in Tibet seven years, during which time he became a tutor to the Dalai Lama; his escape and his time in Tibet are the subject of his book Seven Years in Tibet, which was later filmed with Brad Pitt playing the part of Harrer.

Following his return to Austria in 1952, Harrer took part in a number of moutaineering expeditions; in 1954, he and Fred Beckey made the first ascent of Mount Deborah and Mount Hunter in Alaska and, in 1962, Harrer led a team which made the first ascent of Puncak Jaya, a peak in the Papua Province of Indonesia and the highest peak in Oceania.

Harrer also played golf to a high standard and was Austria's national golf champion in 1958 and 1970.

Harrer died in 2006 at the age of 93.

62. Madonna Harris (1956-), *New Zealand athlete, cyclist, skier and basketball player*

Madonna Harris (nee Gilchrist) was born in Hamilton, New Zealand in 1956.

Harris represented New Zealand in athletics when competing in the 400 metres hurdles in 1977; in the same year, she was also selected to play for New Zealand at basketball.

Following an accident on ice whilst out running, she took up cycling and was selected for the New Zealand cycling team for the 1988 Olympics in Seoul; a puncture in the road race led to her withdrawal and not finishing. Two years later, she was more successful at the Commonwealth Games in Auckland where she won gold in the 3,000 metre individual pursuit and came fourth in the 72 KM road race.

In 1988, she also took part in the Winter Olympics in Calgary, coming in 40th in the 20KM cross-country skiing event.

Since she retired from competitive cycling in 1992 just before the Barcelona Olympics, Harris has taken up endurance horse racing.

Harris was the first New Zealander to have competed in, and remains only one or two New Zealanders to have competed in, both the Summer Olympics and the Winter Olympics.

63. Tony Harris (1916-1993), *South African cricketer and rugby player*

Terence Anthony Harris was born in Kimberley, South Africa in 1916.

Harris's first-class cricket career started in 1933 when, whilst still at school, he scored 114 not out on his debut for Griqualand West in the Currie Cup; by the time he retired in 1949, he had played 55 first-class games, for Griqualand West, Transvaal and South Africa. He played in three Tests for South Africa, all against England; the first two were on the tour to England in 1947, when he played in the first Test which was drawn and the second Test which England won by 10 wickets – in the second Test, he was out in both innings to the bowling of Denis Compton (see Chapter 25); his third and final Test was the drawn fourth Test of England's tour in 1949. In his three Tests, Harris scored 100 runs, with a top score of 60 and an average of 25.

In his 55 first-class matches, Harris scored a total of 3,028 runs, including six centuries and a top score of 191 not out, at an average of 41.47; in his nine overs, he conceded 33 runs but took no wickets.

Harris also played rugby for South Africa at fly-half. He toured with the Springboks to New Zealand in 1937 and played in the second and third Tests, both of which were won by South Africa to give them a 2-1 series win – this is still the only time South Africa have won a series in New Zealand. Harris retained his place in the team for the British Lions tour of 1938, playing in all three Tests. Harris continued his winning streak, winning the first two Tests and, with it, the series; his only try came in the

26-12 win in the first Test; Harris's only defeat as an international rugby player came in the third and final Test, which the Lions won 21-16.

Both Harris's cricket and rugby careers were put on hold during the Second World War, in which he flew spitfires; he was captured in Italy in early 1945 when his plane was shot down.

Harris died in 1993 at the age of 76.

64. Patsy Hendren (1889-1962), *English cricketer and footballer*

Elias Hendren, known throughout the cricket world as "Patsy", was born in Turnham Green, London in 1889.

Hendren started his cricket career with Middlesex in 1907; by the time he retired in 1937, he had scored the third highest number of runs and the second highest number of centuries of any first-class cricketer, despite a career interrupted by the First World War.

His total of 57,611 runs is behind the totals of only Jack Hobbs and Frank Woolley (both of whom also had careers interrupted by the War) and his 170 centuries are only behind the 197 scored by Hobbs. With the bat, he averaged 50.80 and had a highest score of 301 not out; his bowling brought him 47 wickets at an average of 54.76 with a career best of five for 43 but he had much more success as a fielder than a bowler, taking altogether 759 catches, the ninth highest in first-class cricket.

Hendren was first selected to play for England in 1920 and played his last Test in 1935. In his 51 Tests, he scored 3,525 runs, with seven centuries and a top score of 205 not out and an average of 47.63; his runs also included six consecutive 50s in 1928/29, an England record which has since been matched but not beaten. His 7.5 overs bowling in Tests brought him one wicket for 31 runs.

Hendren also played football from 1908 until 1927; he started his career with Queens Park Rangers before moving to Manchester City for the

1908/09 season; after playing two games for Manchester City, he moved to Coventry City for the 1909/10 season, playing in 33 games for them and scoring 14 goals. He then joined Brentford in 1911 and played for them for 16 years. Whilst at Brentford, he was selected to play for England in the Victory International at Ninian Park in 1919, to celebrate the victory of the Allied Forces in the War.

After retiring in 1937, Hendren spent four years coaching cricket at Harrow School before coaching Sussex; later on in life, he became the scorer for Middlesex.

Hendren died in 1962 from Alzheimer's Disease at the age of 73.

65. Rachel Heyhoe-Flint (1939-), *English cricketer and hockey player*

Baroness Heyhoe-Flint was born in Wolverhampton in 1939.

Heyhoe-Flint played in 22 Tests for England at cricket, between 1960 and 1979, captaining the team between 1966 and 1978. In her Test career, she scored 1,594 runs at an average of 45.54, including three centuries and a top score of 179, still the second highest by an Englishwoman; her three Test wickets came at 68 runs per wicket.

Heyhoe-Flint also captained England in the inaugural Women's World Cup in 1973 and went on the play for England in 23 one-day internationals, in which she scored 643 runs, including one century, a score of 114, and averaged 58.45; in the three overs she bowled in ODIs, she took one wicket for 20 runs.

After her retirement from playing cricket, she became, in 1999, one of the first 10 women to be admitted to the MCC and, in 2004, the first women to be elected to the full committee of the MCC.

As well as representing her county Staffordshire at squash and golf, Heyhoe-Flint also played in goal for Staffordshire at hockey for 25 years and was picked to play once for England, in 1964.

Outside sport, Heyhoe-Flint has been a journalist, a broadcaster and an after-dinner speaker, for which, in 1973, she was named Best After-Dinner Speaker by the Guild of Professional Toastmasters.

She has also been a director of Wolverhampton Wanderers Football Club since 1997 and was appointed to the House of Lords in 2011.

66. Alastair Hignell (1955-), *English rugby player and cricketer*

Alastair Hignell was born in Ely, Cambridgeshire, in 1955.

Hignell spent four years at Cambridge University, playing in both the cricket and rugby university teams in each of his four years. He was also only the second person to be appointed captain of both the university cricket and the university rugby teams.

He also played cricket for Gloucestershire and over a ten year cricket career which started in 1974, he scored 7,459 runs, with 11 centuries and a top score of 149 not out, at an average of 29.48. The three wickets he took as a bowler were at a cost of 76.66 for each wicket.

Hignell also played rugby for Bristol but it was whilst he was at university that he received his first call-up to play for England. He was selected as full-back in the game against Australia in Brisbane in 1975, a game which England lost 30-21 after Mike Burton became, in only the fourth minute, the first Englishman to be sent off in an international. Eight days later, Hignell was playing cricket for Gloucestershire against Middlesex.

Hignell played rugby for England 14 times, scoring 48 points for them (three conversions and 14 penalties).

After leaving university, Hignell became a teacher, allowing him to continue with his cricket for Gloucestershire in the summer and his rugby with Bristol in the winter. He later moved into journalism and broadcasting.

In 1999, Hignell was diagnosed with multiple sclerosis. For his contribution to spreading awareness of multiple sclerosis, Hignell won in 2008 the BBC Sports Personality of the Year Helen Rollason Award and, in 2012, his book "Higgy" was voted the best rugby book at the British Sports Book Awards. In 2009, Hignell was awarded the CBE for his services to sport and to charity.

67. Frank Hofle (1967-   ), *German Paralympian skier and cyclist*

Frank Hofle was born in Baden-Wurttemberg, Germany in 1967.

He first competed in the Winter Paralympic Games in 1984, taking part in two of the cross-country skiing events. His first success in the Winter Paralympic Games came four years later when he won gold medal in the two cross-country skiing events in which he took part.

1992 saw Hofle competing in both the Summer Paralympic Games and the Winter Paralympic Games. At the Summer Games that year, he took part in two cycling events, winning gold in one and bronze in the other; at the Winter Games, he took part in the biathlon for the first time, picking up the gold and won two more golds and a silver in his three cross-country skiing events.

The next Winter Paralympic Games were held two years later and he went one better than in 1992, winning gold in the biathlon and three golds and a silver in his four cross-country skiing events.

Hofle competed again at the 1996 Summer Paralympic Games, taking part in two cycling events and winning a bronze medal. This was his last Summer Games but he continued to compete at the Winter Paralympic Games up until 2010. At the 1998 and 2002 Winter Games, he won two more golds in the biathlon and three more golds, another silver and two more bronzes in the cross-country skiing events. The 2006 and 2010 Games brought less success, with Hofle winning just one more silver. By the end though of the 2010 Winter Paralympic Games, Hofle had taken part in 37 events at the Paralympian Games and his medal tally was a total of 14 gold medals of which 10 were in cross-country skiing events and two in each of the biathlon and cycling events, five silver medals, all of which were won in cross-country skiing events and four bronze medals, of which two were for cross-country skiing events and two for cycling.

68. Albert Hornby (1847-1925), *English cricketer, rugby player and footballer*

Albert Hornby was born in Blackburn in 1847.

Hornby played cricket for Cheshire before joining Lancashire, for whom he played from 1867 until 1899. In 1879, Hornby became the first Englishman to represent his country at cricket and rugby when he was selected to play against Australia, in a match Australia won by 10 wickets and a match in which Fred Spofforth took 13 wickets; Hornby only scored 2 and 4 in his two innings and was bowled by Spofforth in each of them.

Hornby was next selected to play for England in 1882 and, in only his second Test, was appointed captain, making him the first man of only two to have ever captained England at both cricket and rugby. Hornby was again twice a victim of Spofforth, bowled for 2 and 9, in a match which Australia won by seven runs and in which Spofforth took 14 wickets. Following England's defeat in this Test, The Sporting Times published its famous obituary of English cricket, which led to England and Australia competing for The Ashes.

Hornby was only selected to play once more for England, in 1884 against Australia. He was captain again in a drawn match but had minimal success, scoring 0 and 4 in his two innings – at least he avoided being bowled by Spofforth; instead, he was stumped by Blackham to the bowling of Boyle in both innings.

In his three Tests, Hornby had only managed a total of 21 runs, failing to get into double figures in any of his six innings. He did however have more success as a bowler – his 28 deliveries conceded no runs and brought him one wicket, to give him the perfect bowling average of 0.

Hornby's first-class career as a batsman was much more successful than his Test career. In total, he played 437 first-class games, scoring a total of 16,109 runs at an average of 24.07; he scored 16 centuries and top-scored with an innings of 188. He only rarely bowled, picking up only 11 wickets altogether at a cost of 23.45 runs per wicket.

Hornby's first rugby club was Preston Grasshoppers, before joining Manchester. His first appearance for England was as a three-quarter in 1877, against Ireland; he played in both England's matches against Scotland and Ireland in 1877 and 1878 but missed the next season due to his cricket taking him overseas. He returned to the England team in 1880 and, in his last match, against Scotland in 1882, was picked as captain. In his nine rugby internationals, he was on the winning side in four of them and the losing side in two of them, the other three being drawn.

Hornby also played a few games of football for Blackburn Rovers, including in their inaugural match against Partick Thistle in January 1878, excelled at boxing and was an outstanding horseman.

Hornby died at the age of 78, in 1925. He had four sons, two of whom pre-deceased him as a result of war wounds, one in the Boer War and the other in the First World War; a third son was awarded the Military Cross in the First World War but died two years after his father's death, exploring in Canada. Hornby's fourth son followed in his father's footsteps, playing a total of 283 matches of cricket for Lancashire between 1899 and 1914.

69. Phil Horne (1960-), *New Zealand cricketer and badminton player*

Phil Horne was born in Wellington, New Zealand in 1960.

Horne played cricket for Auckland and New Zealand. He played three Tests for New Zealand in 1987 and a fourth and final Test in 1990. In his first Test, against the touring West Indians, he scored 9 in the first innings and 0 in the second innings when New Zealand needed only 33 runs to win, a target they reached with only five wickets to spare.

Horne's other three Tests were all overseas, against Sri Lanka and Australia in 1987 and against Pakistan in 1990. In his four Tests, he only managed 71 runs at an average of 10.14 and a top score of 27. Horne hardly fared any better in his four one-day internationals for New Zealand, scoring a total of 50 runs at an average of 12.50, with a top score of 18.

Horne enjoyed more success playing for Auckland; in all his first-class matches, he scored 2,879 runs averaging 34.27 and scoring five centuries with a top score of 209.

Horne also represented New Zealand at badminton and played for them at the Commonwealth Games in Auckland in 1990, but failed to win a medal.

Horne's younger brother, Matt, was also a cricketer and played for New Zealand in 35 Tests between 1996 and 2003.

70. Ken Hough (1928-2009), *New Zealand cricketer and footballer*

Kenneth William Hough was born in Sydney in 1928.

Hough's first taste of international sport was representing Australia at football, when he played in goal for them in four internationals in 1948.

After emigrating to New Zealand, he played cricket for Northern Districts and Auckland and, in 1959, was picked for two Tests against England; although he was picked for his bowling, he scored 62 runs in his two Tests, with a highest score of 31 not out and was only dismissed once, to give him an average of 62 with the bat; with his bowling, he took six wickets to give him a Test average of 29.16 – of his six Test wickets, five were bowled and the sixth was LBW, making Hough the Test bowler with the highest number of Test wickets without any of the dismissals being caught. Altogether, Hough played 28 games of first-class cricket over a career spanning from 1956 to 1960, with his last two games being matches for New Zealand against Australia which were not granted Test status; in his 28 games, he scored 624 runs at an average of 16.42 with a top score of 91 and took 169 wickets at an average of 20.87, with best figures of seven for 43, in a match in which his overall figures were 12 for 146; in 1958/59, he helped Auckland win the Plunket Shield, with his 36 wickets at an average of 12.13.

After moving to New Zealand, Hough kept up with his football and, in 1958, played in five international matches for New Zealand, the first of which was against Australia, the country he had represented ten years earlier.

After his last game of cricket for New Zealand in 1960, Hough went back to live in Australia and played for the New South Wales Country XI against the 1965/66 England touring team; he also played some rugby league, at which he represented Papua New Guinea. Hough therefore has the rare distinction of being a sportsman who has not only played one sport for two countries but also two sports for one country and the even rarer distinction, and perhaps even a unique one, of playing three different sports for three different countries.

Hough died in 2009 at the age of 80.

71. David Houghton (1957-), *Zimbabwean cricketer and hockey player*

David Houghton was born in 1957 in Bulowayo, in what is now Zimbabwe.

Houghton is the youngest of three brothers, all of whom played sport; his oldest brother Ken played hockey for Zimbabwe and his second brother played first-class cricket for Rhodesia B.

David also played hockey for Zimbabwe for several years and was regarded by Kallimullah, the Pakistan captain, as the greatest goalkeeper he ever played against. He is however better known as a cricketer.

Houghton's first-class cricket career started when he was 21, when he played for Rhodesia in the Currie Cup. It was not until he was 35 though that Zimbabwe was granted Test status; he captained them in their first four Tests and, when making a century in the first Test, became only the second man, after Charles Bannerman for Australia in the very first Test back in 1877, to score a century as captain in his country's inaugural Test. In his 22 Tests between 1992 and 1997, he scored a total of 1,464 runs at an average of 43.05; he scored four centuries, including a top score of 266, which remains the highest Test score by a Zimbabwean. His total of 1,464 runs is the highest by any batsman without scoring a duck. He did not concede a run in the five balls he bowled in Test cricket nor did he pick up a wicket.

Houghton also played in 63 one-day internationals for Zimbabwe, captaining them in 17 of them. In his ODIs, he scored 1,530 runs at an average of 26.37, with one century, a score of 142 in a World Cup game against New Zealand; in the two overs he bowled in ODIs, he took one wicket for 19 runs. In all first-class cricket, Houghton played 120 games, scoring 7,445 runs at an average of 39.39, with 17 centuries and his highest score being his Test score of 266; his two wickets as a bowler came at a cost of 59 per wicket.

After retiring from cricket at the age of 40, Houghton became a commentator; he has also coached Worcestershire, Derbyshire and the Zimbabwe team.

72. Scott Huey (1923-2012), *Irish cricketer, badminton player and hockey player*

Samuel Scott Johnson Huey was born in County Donegal in 1923.

He played cricket for Ireland 36 times between 1951 and 1966, as a right-hand batsman and a left-arm orthodox spin bowler, captaining them on five occasions; 20 of his matches were first-class fixtures and, although he had little success with the bat, scoring only 134 runs in these 20 matches at an average of 5.15, he enjoyed much more success with the ball, taking 66 wickets at an average of 18.22. His best bowling analysis came when he played for Ireland against the MCC in 1954, when he took six for 49 in the first innings and eight for 48 in the second innings, giving him the best bowling analysis of any Irish bowler – in the same match he scored 23 not out with the bat, his highest score.

Huey also has the distinction of being the last bowler to claim the wicket of Len Hutton, when Hutton was stumped for 89 off the bowling of Huey when playing in his farewell match for the MCC against Ireland in 1960.

As well as representing Ireland at cricket, Huey also represented them at badminton; he also represented Ulster at hockey.

By profession, Huey was a pharmaceutical sales director and, after retiring from cricket, became a national selector.

Huey died in 2012 at the age of 88.

73. Clara Hughes (1972-   ), *Canadian cyclist and speed skater*

Clara Hughes was born in Winnipeg in 1972.

Hughes started speed skating at the age of 16 but, by the time she was 17, cycling became a priority. She represented Canada in the cycling events at the 1996 Olympics in Atlanta, the 2000 Olympics in Sydney and the 2012 Olympics in London. Her medal tally at these Games consists of the two bronze medals she won in 1996; since then, in cycling events, she has won a gold medal at the 2002 Commonwealth Games, a gold medal at the 2003 Pan American Games and two gold medals at the Pan American Championships in 2011.

Although cycling had taken over her life at 17, Hughes never gave up on her speed skating and, as well as competing in cycling events at the Summer Olympics, she has also competed in the speed skating events at the Winter Olympics. After winning the bronze medal in the 5,000 metre event at the 2002 Winter Olympics, Hughes won the gold in 2006 and the bronze again in 2010 – at the 2010 Winter Olympic Games, Hughes was the flag bearer for the Canadian team. After winning the silver medal in the 5,000 metre event at the 2003 World Championships, she won the gold medal at the 2004 World Championships, the bronze in 2005 and the silver medal again in 2008 and 2009.

Having struggled with depression in the past, Hughes is now involved in charities concerned with mental health and in staging cycling events across Canada to raise awareness about mental health.

74. Geoff Hurst (1941-   ), *English footballer and cricketer*

Sir Geoffrey Hurst was born in Ashton-under-Lyne in 1941.

Hurst is best known for his performances as a footballer but, in his early 20s, he played cricket for Essex as well. In 1962, he played in his only first-class game, against Lancashire. Although Essex won the match, Hurst's contribution was minimal – he scored 0 not out in the first innings and was bowled for a duck in the second; at least he had more success in the field, where he held on to two catches.

This performance on debut did not put him off cricket and he continued to play for the Essex 2nd XI, playing 23 games for them between 1962 and 1964 before deciding to concentrate solely on his football.

Hurst first joined West Ham United in 1959 and over 14 years, made 411 appearances and scored 180 goals for them; whilst at West Ham, he won the F. A. Cup in 1964 and the European Cup Winners Cup in 1965. In 1972, he moved to Stoke City and, during his three seasons with them, he played 108 games for them, scoring 30 goals. In 1975, he moved to West Bromwich Albion, for whom he played 10 games and scored two goals.

Hurst also had stints with Cape Town City, Cork Celtic and finally with Seattle Sounders before hanging up his boots in 1976.

Hurst's greatest exploits as a footballer came at the 1966 World Cup. He was not selected for the three group stage games but was picked for the quarter-final against Argentina, a game in which he scored the only goal. He retained his place in the win over Portugal in the semi-final and in the final against West Germany, despite Jimmy Greaves, whom he had replaced for the game against Argentina following an injury, being fit again. His hat-trick in the final which England won 4-2 remains the only hat-trick scored in a World Cup Final and his second goal remains, after Maradona's "Hand of God" goal in the 1986 World Cup finals, perhaps the most talked about goal of the World Cup finals – the goal was awarded by the Russian linesman after his shot in extra time bounced down off the underside of the crossbar, although there appears to be no conclusive evidence to show whether or not the ball did actually cross the line after hitting the crossbar. His third goal resulted in one of the most memorable pieces of match commentary, Kenneth Wolstenholme's "there are some people on the pitch .. they think it is all over .. it is now", as Hurst's powerful left foot shot flew into the net in the dying seconds of the game.

Hurst continued to play for England until 1972. He played in three of England's four games at the 1970 World Cup and by the time he retired, he had played 49 games and scored 24 goals for England.

After retiring from football, Hurst tried his hand at club management, first with Telford and then, from 1979 until 1981, with Chelsea. Hurst was awarded an MBE in 1975 and was knighted in 1998, for services to football.

75. Bo Jackson (1962-　), *American baseball player, American footballer and basketball player*

Vincent Jackson was born in Alabama in 1962; he acquired the nickname "Bo" following his appearance alongside the musician Bo Diddley in an advertising campaign run by Nike.

In 1982, Jackson went to Auburn University on a football (American football) scholarship; whilst at university, he won the Heisman Trophy, awarded each year to the most outstanding collegiate football player in the US.

In 1987, he signed up for the Los Angeles Raiders, after rejecting an offer from the Tampa Bay Buccaneers whom he believed wanted to prevent him from playing baseball. During his four years with the Los Angeles Raiders, he scored 16 touchdowns and in 1990, the year in which he scored five touchdowns in 10 games, he was named in the US All-Star team. A serious hip injury in early 1991 whilst playing against the Cincinnati Bengals put an end to his American football career.

By turning down the Tampa Bay Buccaneers, Jackson was able to continue playing baseball, playing for the Kansas City Royals from 1986 until his injury in 1991. In 1989, the year in which he had a career best with 32 home runs, he was named in baseball's American League All-Star team – his inclusion in the American Football All-Star team a year later made him the first American to be named in All-Star teams in two major US sports.

Following his injury playing football, Jackson was released by the Kansas City Royals and tried his hand at basketball; after playing a few games of basketball for a semi-pro team in Los Angeles, Jackson resumed his baseball career with the Chicago White Sox, for whom he played for two seasons.

Following his retirement from pro sport in 1994, Jackson completed his university studies and graduated; since then, he has made a number of appearances in television shows and in films, as well as being president of the Sports Medicine Council.

In 2013, ESPN Sport Science named Jackson as the greatest athlete of all time.

76. Asif Karim (1963-), *Kenyan cricketer and tennis player*

Asif Karim was born in Mombasa in 1963.

Karim played cricket for Kenya in their first 25 one-day internationals, from 1980 until 2003. He took part in the World Cup in 1996, in 1999 (when he was captain) and in 2003, when Kenya became the first non-Test playing country to reach the semi-finals.

Karim batted right-handed and bowled slow left-arm orthodox; in his 25 ODIs, he scored a total of 228 runs at an average of 12.66 with a top score of 53 and took 27 wickets at an average of 41.25. His best performance came in one of the group stage matches in 2003, when his bowling analysis was 8.2 overs, six maidens, three wickets for seven runs against the eventual winners Australia; although these figures were not enough to bring Kenya a victory, they were enough to earn Karim the man-of-the-match award.

Karim also represented Kenya at tennis in the Davis Cup. His only appearance was against Egypt in 1988, when he played two singles matches, both of which he lost in straight sets and in the doubles match, which he lost in four sets.

77. Roswitha Krause (1949-   ), *German swimmer and handball player*

Roswitha Krause was born in Dahme in what was then in East Germany, in 1949.

Krause represented East Germany at the 1968 Olympics in Mexico City, winning a silver medal in the 4 x 100 metres freestyle relay event. Although she continued swimming after her appearance at the Olympics, winning national titles through to the late 1970s, she turned her attention more to handball. She was a member of the East Germany handball team at both the 1976 Olympics in Montreal and the 1980 Olympics in Moscow, winning the silver medal in 1976 and the bronze medal in 1980. With the East German team, she also won two world titles at handball, the first in 1975 and the second in 1978.

Her success at the 1976 Olympics made Krause the first woman to win Olympic medals in two different sports.

After the 1980 Olympics, she became the swimming and handball coach at Humboldt University.

78. Trevor Laughlin (1951-   ), *Australian cricketer, hockey player and Australian rules footballer*

Trevor Laughlin was born in Nyah West, Victoria, Australia in 1951.

Laughlin played cricket for Victoria as an all-rounder batting left –handed and bowling right-arm medium pace, his first-class cricket career lasting from 1974 until 1981; during part of this period, a number of Australian cricketers were not available for selection for the national team as they had committed to Kerry Packer's World Cricket Series matches and, as a consequence, Laughlin found himself selected to play in three Test matches in 1978 and 1979, two against the West Indies and one against England. In his three Tests, Laughlin scored 87 runs at an average of 17.40 with a top score of 34 and took six wickets at an average of 43.66. He also played for Australia in six one-day internationals, scoring 105 runs at an average of 26.25, with a top score of 74 and taking eight wickets at an average of 28.00. Laughlin played a total of 58 first-class cricket matches, scoring 2,770 runs at an average of 32.58 with one century to his name, a score of 113 and taking 99 wickets at an average of 31.92, with best bowling figures of five for 38.

As well as being an international cricketer, Laughlin also played hockey for Australia and Australian rules football for Mordialloc Football Club.

Laughlin's son Ben has also played five one-day internationals for Australia.

79. Katrin Lehmann (1980-   ), *Swiss footballer and ice hockey player*

Katrin Lehmann was born in Zurich in 1980 and is a Swiss footballer and ice hockey player.

Lehmann was a member of Switzerland's ice hockey team at the 2006 Winter Olympics; Switzerland lost their three group stage games but beat Italy convincingly to take 7th place; Lehmann scored three of Switzerland's goals at the Games. Four years later, she was captain of the Swiss ice hockey team for the 2010 Winter Olympics; after losing group stage games to the eventual winners Canada and to Sweden, Switzerland finished in fifth place after beating Russia in the game to decide fifth and sixth places; Lehmann scored two of Switzerland's goals at the 2010 Games. She also played ice hockey for the Swedish team AIK IF and was a forward in the team which won the International Ice Hockey Federation's European Women's Champions Cup in 2008; it was AIK IF's fourth consecutive win.

A year after winning the European Ice Hockey Champions Cup, she was the substitute goalkeeper for the German football club FCR 2001 Duisberg, for the first leg of the UEFA Women's Club Championship final against the Russian team Zvevda – 2005; FCR 2001 Duisberg won the first leg 6-0 and drew the second leg 1-1, making Lehmann the first woman to be involved in two European club finals in different sports.

80. Terje Loevaas (1957-   ), *Norwegian Paralympian skier and athlete*

Terje Loevaas was born in 1957 in the Norwegian region of Drammen.

Loevaas won medals at the Summer Paralympic Games from 1984 until 1992 and medals at the Winter Paralympic Games from 1980 until 1994.

Loevaas had more success at the Winter Games, where he won all of his 10 gold medals, in cross-country skiing events. His most successful Games were his last, in 1994, when he won four gold medals, to add to the three he won in 1984, the two he won in 1980 and the one in 1988. He also won two silver medals at the Winter Games, one in 1980 and the other in 1988.

At the Summer Games, Loevaas's competed in athletics events, over 1,500 metres and 5,000 metres. Over the 5,000 metre distance, he won a bronze medal in the 1984, 1988 and 1992 Games, but went one better at the 1988 and 1992 Games over the 1,500 metre distance, when he won a silver at both Games.

By the time Loevaas finished competing in the Paralympics Games, he had won 10 gold medals and three silver medals at the Winter Games in cross-country skiing events and two silver medals and three bronze medals in athletics events at the Summer Games.

81. Christa Luding (1959-   ), *German speed skater and cyclist*

Christa Luding (nee Rothenburger) was born in 1959 in Weisswasser, in what was then in East Germany. She is one of a few athletes to have competed in and won medals at both the Summer and Winter Olympics.

Luding won her first gold medal at the Olympics at the Winter Games in 1984 in Sarajevo, representing East Germany, in the 500 metre speed skating event. Four years later, at the Winter Games in Calgary, she came second in the speed skating event over 500 metres but won the gold in the 1,000 metre event. In 1992, at the Winter Games in Albertville, this time representing Germany after its unification, she won the bronze medal in the 500 metre speed skating event.

Luding also enjoyed success as a speed skater at the World Championships, being the World Champion in 1985 and 1988 and runner-up in 1986 and 1989. She also won four gold medals at World Cup events between 1986 and 1989.

Encouraged by her coach (whom subsequently she married) to take up cycling when not speed skating, Luding reached a standard that enabled her to compete in international cycling competitions and, by 1986, was good enough to win gold at the track cycling speed event at the World Cycling Championships, making her only the second woman to be a World Champion at both cycling and speed skating.

In 1988, she competed in the Summer Olympics in Seoul, where she won the silver medal in the 1,000 metre sprint in track cycling, making her the only athlete to have won medals at the Summer Games and the Winter Games in the same year, a record which, unless the scheduling of the Games changes, will now never be beaten as they are no longer held in the same year.

82. Alfred Lyttelton (1859-1915), *English cricketer and footballer*

The Hon Alfred Lyttelton was born in 1859, in Westminster, the twelfth and last child of the 4th Baron Lyttelton and his first wife.

Whilst at Cambridge University, Lyttelton played in Varsity matches against Oxford University in five sports, namely cricket, football, athletics, real tennis and rackets. By playing in Varsity matches in five different sports, Lyttelton matched the achievement a few years earlier of fellow Old Etonian Cuthbert Ottaway, who had represented Oxford University in the same five sports in which Lyttelton represented Cambridge; Ottaway went in to become the first captain of England at football.

Whilst at university, Lyttelton also played football for the Old Etonians in the 1876 F. A. Cup Final which they lost to Wanderers in a replay after the first game was drawn. A year later, he was picked to play football for England against Scotland, a game in which he scored England's only goal in a 3-1 defeat.

After graduating, Lyttelton played cricket for Middlesex. By the time he retired from playing first-class cricket in 1887, having played in 101 first-class matches, he had scored 4,429 runs at an average of 27.85, with seven centuries to his name and a top score of 181; as a wicketkeeper, he held on to 134 catches and made 70 stumpings.

By 1880, Lyttelton was selected to play cricket for England, making him the first man to be selected for England at both football and cricket. Over the next four years, he played in four Tests, all against Australia, in which he scored 94 runs at an average of 15.66, with a top score of 31. His most memorable performance was during the Test against Australia at the Oval in 1884 when, with Australia having scored 500 runs for only six wickets, Lyttelton was asked by his captain, Lord Harris, to remove his wicketkeeping pads and gloves, with Dr W. G. Grace (see Chapter 55) replacing him behind the stumps, and try his hand at bowling; after eight overs of bowling under-arm, Lyttelton had dismissed the last four Australian batsmen for 19 runs, giving him a bowling average of 4.75 in Tests - the only wickets he took in all first-class cricket were the four he took in this innings.

Five of Lyttelton's brothers also played first-class cricket and his brother, Edward, also played one game of football for England, as well as in the same F. A. Cup Final as Alfred.

Away from sport, Lyttelton entered the law and politics. He was elected to the House of Commons in 1895 as a Liberal Unionist and served as the Secretary of State for the Colonies between 1903 and 1905.

Following an injury whilst playing cricket in South Africa in 1913, Lyttelton returned to England where he was diagnosed with having an abscess in his stomach; an unsuccessful attempt to remove it led to his death that year at the age of 56.

83. Jack MacBryan (1892-1983), *English cricketer and hockey player*

John Crawford William MacBryan was born in Wiltshire in 1892.

MacBryan first played first-class cricket for Somerset in 1911 but his cricket was interrupted by the First World War, in which he was wounded and captured at the battle of Le Cateau in August 1914, remaining a prisoner-of-war until the War ended four years later. After the War, he went up to Cambridge University, winning his blue at cricket in 1920.

In 1920, he was also picked as a member of the Great Britain hockey team for the Olympics in Antwerp. The Great Britain team was actually the England team and they won the gold medal by beating Denmark 5-1 and Belgium 12-1 - they were awarded a walkover by France, who were the only other country taking part and who had been beaten 9-1 by Denmark; MacBryan played in the match against Belgium.

After graduating, MacBryan continued to play cricket for Somerset and was their leading batsman in the first half of the 1920s. This led to him being selected to play for England in 1924 against the touring South African team for the Test at Old Trafford; the match was scheduled to be played over three days but rain fell on the first day with the South Africans having scored 116 for 4 and further rain on the second and third days prevented any further play – in his one and only Test, MacBryan neither batted nor bowled nor took a catch, making him the only Test cricketer never to have scored a run and never to have taken a wicket or a catch.

MacBryan played for Somerset until 1936 and, by the time he retired, had played 206 games of first-class cricket, scoring 10,322 runs at an average of 29.49, including 18 centuries and a top score of 164.

MacBryan was a member of Sunningdale and Prince's at Sandwich and played golf to a handicap of four; he also represented Richmond at rugby.

MacBryan died in 1983 at the age of 90; immediately prior to his death, MacBryan was England's oldest living Test cricketer.

84. Gregor Macgregor (1869-1919), *Scottish cricketer and rugby player*

Gregor Macgregor was born in Edinburgh in 1869.

Macgregor attended Cambridge University and played in Varsity matches in both cricket and rugby.

His career as a first-class cricketer spanned almost 20 years, starting in 1888. He never bowled in first-class cricket but, in his 265 games, he scored 6,381 runs at an average of 18.02, with three centuries and a highest score of 141. It was his ability as a wicketkeeper though which earned him selection in the England team; in all first-class matches, he took 411 catches and made 148 stumpings.

He played in eight Tests in total, between 1890 and 1893; he only scored 96 runs in Tests at an average 12 with a top score of 31 but, behind the stumps, took 14 catches and made three stumpings.

1890 also saw him selected to play rugby for Scotland, as well as an original member of the newly-formed Barbarians rugby club; Macgregor played in all three of Scotland's Home Nations Championships (now, with the addition of France and Italy, the Six Nations) in 1890, 1891 1893 and 1894, missing the 1892 Championships because of his participation in the Ashes tour to Australia that year. He played his 13th and last international for Scotland in 1896. In his 13 internationals, in which he played either full-back or as a three –quarter, Scotland won eight of the matches, lost four and drew one. Macgregor scored one try, against Ireland in 1891 and two conversions, against England in 1891, the year Scotland won all three of their Home Nations fixtures.

After graduation, Macgregor worked at the London Stock Exchange. He died in 1919, just before what would have been his 50th birthday.

85. Kenneth Macleod (1888-1967), *Scottish rugby player, athlete, cricketer, footballer and golfer*

Kenneth Macleod was born in Dunmartonshire.

Whilst at Fettes College and still only 17, Macleod was picked to play for Scotland at rugby against New Zealand, a match the All Blacks won 12-7. After leaving school, he went to Cambridge University where, as well as playing in the university rugby team, he played in the cricket Varsity match as well as, as a 100 yards sprinter and as a long jumper, in the athletics Varsity match; it is claimed that, at the time, he held the Scottish long jump record.

Whilst at university, Macleod continued to play for Scotland at rugby; however at the age of 21, at the request of his father, following serious injuries to two of his brothers whilst playing rugby, he gave the game up. Overall, he played 10 matches for Scotland, winning six of them and losing four. He scored a total of 25 points, with two conversions, two penalties and a goal scored from a mark, as well as four tries, including two in his final game against England which Scotland won 16-10.

After retiring from rugby, Macleod played cricket for Lancashire between 1908 and 1913. By the time he retired from cricket, he had played 94 games of first-class cricket, scoring 3,458 runs at an average of 23.84 and taking 103 wickets at an average of 26.62; his six centuries included a best score of 131 and his best bowling analysis was six for 29.

Whilst playing cricket for Lancashire, Macleod lived in Manchester and, whilst there, played football for Manchester City, although there is no record of him making any appearances for the first team.

In later life, Macleod emigrated to South Africa where he enjoyed success in a fifth sport, becoming the Natal amateur golf champion. Macleod died in South Africa in 1967 at the age of 79.

86. Norman Mair (1928-2014), *Scottish rugby player and cricketer*

Norman Mair was born in Edinburgh in 1928.

In 1951, he played rugby for Scotland as hooker in their four Home Nations fixtures that year and, although three of the matches were lost, Scotland had the satisfaction of beating a Wales team, including 11 British Lions, 17-0.

A year later, Mair played his only game of cricket for Scotland, in a match against Worcestershire; the three-day match, which was drawn, was badly affected by rain and, in his only innings in the match, Mair scored 4 not out.

Away from playing sport, Mair wrote about it and became the Scotsman chief rugby writer in 1962 and, in 1994, Mair was awarded the MBE. When Mair died in 2014 at the age of 86 after suffering from Alzheimer's, Sir Ian McGeechan described him as "the best rugby writer of them all, without question".

87. Harry Makepeace (1881-1952), *English cricketer and footballer*

Joseph William Henry Makepeace was born in Middlesbrough in 1881.

Makepeace first signed for Everton Football Club in 1902 and, after making his debut in 1903, went on to play 336 games for them, scoring 23 goals. In 1906, he was picked to play for England against Scotland, a fixture he played in again in 1910 and 1912; he was also selected to play against Wales in 1912.

By the time he played his last game for Everton in 1915, he had played in their F. A. Cup winning team of 1906, when they beat Newcastle United and in their League Championship winning team of 1914/15; he also played in the 1907 F. A. Cup Final when Everton were runners-up to Sheffield Wednesday.

Makepeace also played cricket for Lancashire. He first played for them in 1906 and continued playing for them until 1930, winning the County Championship with them three years in succession from 1926. By the time he retired, he had played in 499 games of first-class cricket, scoring 25,799 runs at an average of 36.23, with 43 centuries and a top score of 203 to his name. His legbreaks brought him 42 wickets at 46.92 apiece, with a best bowling analysis of four for 33.

Makepeace was picked for the Ashes tour to Australia in 1920/21. After England were heavily beaten in the first Test, Makepeace was selected for the other four Test matches, all of which England also lost, to give Australia their first 5-0 whitewash in an Ashes series. In his four Tests, Makepeace scored 279 runs at an average of 34.87, with a top score of 117, his only Test century.

After retiring from football, Makepeace stayed with Everton on their coaching staff and after retiring from cricket, stayed with Lancashire on their coaching staff.

As well as being one of only 12 Englishmen who have played both football and cricket for England, he remains the only Englishman to have won the County Championship at cricket and the League Championship and F. A. Cup at football.

In his book The Roses Matches 1919-1939, the cricket writer Neville Cardus counted Makepeace amongst the immortals of Lancashire and Yorkshire cricket. Makepeace died in 1952 at the age of 71.

88. Nick Mallett (1956-   ), *South African rugby player and cricketer*

Nick Mallett was born in Haileybury, England in 1956 but moved to Rhodesia soon after he was born, when his father took up a teaching post there.

After graduating from the University of Cape Town, he spent two years at Oxford University, winning a blue at both cricket and rugby. Over the two years he was at Oxford, he played 11 matches at cricket for them, scoring 237 runs at an average of 13.17 and with a top score of 52 and taking 19 wickets at an average of 44.26; his highlight though came in the match against Somerset in 1980 when he hit Ian Botham (see Chapter 16) for three 6s in one over – it should be noted though that Botham was only bowling off-breaks rather than medium fast with which he had more success.

In 1984, Mallett was picked as South Africa's number 8 in two matches against the visiting South America team. Both matches were won by South Africa, with Mallett scoring a try in the first match.

Since retiring as a player, Mallett has coached a number of clubs and, in 1997, was appointed coach of the South African team, which, whilst he was coach, won a record-equalling 17 consecutive Test matches. More recently, he coached Italy at a time which saw them record victories over Scotland and France in the Six Nations Championships.

89. Roberto Marson (1944-2011), *Italian Paralympian athlete, fencer and swimmer*

Roberto Marson was born in Italy in 1944.

When chopping a tree which fell on his back, Marson lost the use of his legs and, as a consequence, was able to take part in the Paralympic Games.

Marson's first Paralympic Games were in 1964 in Tokyo, where he competed in athletics events and fencing events, winning two gold medals and two silver medals in discus and javelin events and one gold medal and two silver medals in fencing events.

Four years later, in Tel Aviv, he was even more successful, winning three gold medals in athletic events, two gold medals in swimming events and four gold medals and two silver medals in fencing events; his performances in 1968 earned him recognition as the outstanding athlete of the 1972 Paralympic Games.

Marson also participated in the fencing events at the Paralympic Games in 1972 and in 1976, winning three golds and two silvers in 1972 and a bronze medal in 1976. His final tally of medals at Paralympic Games was 16 gold medals (five for athletics, eight for fencing and three for swimming), eight silver medals (two for athletics and six for fencing) and one bronze medal (for fencing).

After his Paralympic Games days were over, Marson was President of the Italian Federation for Handicapped Sports from 1980 until 1990.

Marson died in 2011 at the age of 67.

90. Brian McKechnie (1953-   ), *New Zealand rugby player and cricketer*

Brian McKechnie was born in 1953, in Southland, New Zealand.

Between 1977 and 1981, McKechnie played as a three-quarter or full-back for New Zealand in 26 matches including 10 international matches. His 10 international games included the games against England, Wales and Scotland which New Zealand won when winning their first Grand Slam over the Home Nations in 1978. The win against Wales was not without controversy, with Andy Haden diving out of a line-out with New Zealand losing 10-12 and little more than a minute to play; a penalty was awarded and up-stepped McKechnie to score the penalty which gave New

Zealand a 13-12 victory, thereby denying Wales a rare win over the All Blacks. In his 10 Test matches, seven of which were won by New Zealand, McKechnie scored 46 points, made up of 11 penalties, five conversions and a drop goal.

McKechnie also represented New Zealand at cricket in 14 one day internationals, including playing for them in the 1975 and 1979 World Cups. In his 14 ODIs, he scored 54 runs at an average of 13.50 and with a top score of 27; his bowling brought him 19 wickets at an average of 26.05, with best bowling figures of three for 23. His last ODI was in 1981 and, because of one incident, is as memorable as the Wales rugby game he played in; with New Zealand needing six runs to tie the match against Australia, Trevor Chappell bowled a "grubber" (an under-arm ball along the ground) to McKechnie at the far end, thereby denying him any realistic opportunity to tie the match. This was considered contrary to the traditions of the game and the incident was described by the New Zealand Prime Minister as an act of cowardice and by the chairman of the New Zealand Cricket Council as the worst sporting action he had ever seen. No doubt many in Wales, where they tend to be more passionate about their rugby than their cricket, took a slightly different view.

By the time McKechnie retired from cricket in 1986, he had played 50 first-class games for Otago, scoring 1,169 runs at an average of 18.26, with a highest score of 51 and taking 100 wickets at an average of 30.65 with best figures of four for 24.

After retiring from cricket, McKechnie served on New Zealand's national selection panel.

91. Roy McLean (1930-2007), *South African cricketer and rugby player*

Roy McLean was born in Pietermaritzburg, South Africa, in 1930.

Having been outstanding at cricket, hockey and rugby at school, McLean first played cricket for Natal in 1949 and, between 1951 and 1964, played in 40 Tests for South Africa. He played a total of 200 matches of first-class cricket, scoring 10,969 runs at an average of 36.68, with 22 centuries and a highest score of 207; his two wickets bowling cost 244 runs.

In Tests, McLean scored 2,120 runs at an average of 30.28, with five centuries and a top score of 142, which he made against England at Lord's, in the second Test of the 1955 South African tour – during this innings, he dominated the scoring, scoring 142 out of 196 runs scored whilst he was at the crease. His most memorable Test innings came though in 1953 when he scored 76 not out against Australia in Melbourne to win the match for South Africa and draw the series; Australia had scored 520 in their first innings but South Africa needed 295 in the fourth innings of the match to win the Test and level the series; McLean came to the crease at 191 for 4 and, after he was dropped first ball, McLean and his captain Jack Cheetham put on 106, with McLean scoring 76 of them, to win the match by six wickets.

McLean also toured England with the South Africans in 1960 but he was one of only two of the tourists to perform well on the tour. A year later, he returned to England with an unofficial team, consisting of eight future South African cricketers, many of whom were to be part of the team which was to become the best in the world in the late 1960s, before the boycotting of South Africa from competing in international sport because of its apartheid regime.

McLean also played rugby for Natal at fly-half. He proved to be a thorn in the side of Australia at rugby as well as cricket when, in 1953, he scored a drop goal with only seconds remaining to secure a 15-14 victory.

After retiring from cricket in 1966, McLean became an insurance salesman. He died in 2007 at the age of 77.

92. Edwin McLeod (1900-1989), *New Zealand cricketer and hockey player*

Edwin McLeod was born in Auckland in 1900.

McLeod played first-class cricket for Auckland from 1920 until 1924 and for Wellington from 1925 until 1941. Although his first-class career spanned 16 years, he only played 28 first-class games, one of which was the second Test against England in 1930. In his one Test, McLeod scored 16 and 2 not out with the bat and bowled two overs for five runs without taking a wicket in a drawn match. In all his first-class matches, McLeod scored 1,407 runs at an average of 32.72 with a top score of 102, his only century; with the ball, he took 20 wickets at an average of 33.20.

Before being selected to play cricket for New Zealand, McLeod had already played for his country at hockey, when captaining them in 1922 in their first ever international, a game against Australia which New Zealand won 5-4. McLeod was still captaining the team 13 years later when they played against the touring Indian team which won all three of the international matches played between the two countries – India were warming up for the Olympics in 1936, where they won the gold medal.

After retiring from playing hockey, McLeod became a national selector for the hockey team.

McLeod died in 1989 at the age of 88.

93. Don McRae (1914-1986), *New Zealand cricketer and footballer*

Don McRae was born in Christchurch, New Zealand in 1914.

McRae first played cricket for Canterbury in the 1937/38 season and, in 1946, was picked to play for New Zealand against the touring Australians. In New Zealand's first innings, Mc Rae was out second ball for a duck, in their total of 42 and, in the second innings scored 8 out a total of 54; in his 14 overs, he took no wickets and conceded 44 runs, in a match which Australia won easily, by an innings and 103 runs. The 295 runs scored in this match is the third lowest aggregate number of runs scored in a completed Test match.

After the Test, McRae never played first-class cricket again but by then, in a career interrupted by the War, he had played 17 first-class games of cricket, scoring 354 runs at an average of 15.39 with a highest score of 43 and taking 56 wickets at an average of 22.51 with best figures of five for 20.

In the same year as he played his only Test cricket match, McRae made his only appearance for New Zealand at football; as with the cricket, Australia won the match easily, a 7-1 thrashing and, with McRae in goal, it comes as little surprise that he was not picked again.

McRae died in 1986 at the age of 72.

94. Arthur Milton (1928-2007), *English cricketer and footballer*

Clement Arthur Milton was born in Bristol in 1928.

Milton attended Cotham Grammar School where he was captain of the football, rugby and cricket teams. He first played cricket for Gloucestershire in 1948 and, by the time he retired in 1974, had played 620 first-class games. Although he was picked as twelfth man for the 1953 Ashes series, it was not until 1958 that Milton played his first game for England. His first Test was against New Zealand and he opened the batting with M. J. K. Smith (see Chapter 133) who was already a dual international, having played rugby for England as well - coincidentally Milton remains the last Englishman to have played cricket and football for England and Smith the last Englishman to have played cricket and rugby for England. Milton's first Test also saw him become the first Englishman to spend the whole of a Test match on the pitch – New Zealand batted first and were bowled out for 67; Milton opened the batting for England, who declared on 267 for 2 with Milton 104 not out, having put on 194 in an unbroken partnership with the England captain Peter May; England then bowled out the New Zealanders a second time for 129 to win the match by an innings and 71 runs.

Milton played in six Tests for England, scoring 204 runs at an average of 25.50. He only scored the one century, the innings of 104 not out on his debut; the four balls be bowled in Test cricket cost 12 runs without a wicket. His last Test was against India in 1959. In his 620 games of first-class cricket, he scored 32,150 runs at an average of 33.63, with 56 centuries and a highest score of 170 to his name; his right-arm medium pace bowling brought him 79 wickets at a cost of 46.07 apiece.

Milton signed for Arsenal just after the War but only made his debut in the first team in 1951; not long after, he was picked for the national team and played in 2-2 draw against Austria at Wembley in November 1951 – this turned out to be his only football game for England. He continued playing for Arsenal until 1955, helping them win the League Championship in 1952/53. By the time of his move to Bristol City in early 1955, Milton had played 84 games for Arsenal and scored 21 goals for them. At Bristol City, he helped them win promotion to the Second Division at the end of the 1954/55 season but he retired from football after having played 15 games for Bristol City, to concentrate on his cricket.

After retiring from first class cricket, Milton coached the Oxford University team before becoming a postman. He died in 2007 at the age of 79.

95. William Milton (1854-1930), *English rugby player and South African cricketer*

Sir William Milton was born in Little Marlow, Buckinghamshire in 1854.

Milton played rugby as a three-quarter and was picked to play for England in two internationals, against Scotland in 1874 and 1875. Although Milton did not score any points, England won both games, the first by one goal to nil and the second by two goals to nil, at a time when matches were decided by the number of goals (i.e. converted tries) scored.

Milton emigrated to South Africa at the age of 24, where he played six first-class games of cricket, three of which were for South Africa. The three Tests in which Milton played were South Africa's first three Test matches, the first two against England when they toured South Africa in 1888/89 and the third, which Milton captained, when England returned in 1891/92.

All three Tests resulted in heavy losses for South Africa, with John Briggs taking, in Milton's second Test, seven wickets for 17 runs in the first innings and eight wickets for 11 in the second innings; Briggs's 15 wickets for 28 runs is the sixth best bowling analysis of all time in Test cricket.

In his three Tests, Milton scored only 68 runs, at an average of 11.33 and a highest score of 21; with his bowling, he took two wickets for 48 runs. His first-class figures were not much better, with 152 runs scored at an average of 13.81 and a top score of 47, whilst his best bowling figures were four for 63.

Before the turn of the century, Milton moved to Southern Rhodesia (now Zimbabwe) and, in 1901, was appointed Administrator of Southern Rhodesia, a position he held until 1914 before retiring on the grounds of declining health.

Milton had two sons, Cecil and John (known as Jumbo). Both played rugby for England, Jumbo in five games between 1904 and 1907 and Cecil in one game in 1906; Jumbo also played two games of first-class cricket when he returned to live in South Africa.

Milton died in 1930 at the age of 75.

96. Frank Mitchell (1872-1935), *English cricketer and rugby player*

Frank Mitchell was born in 1872 in Market Weighton, Yorkshire.

Mitchell's first-class cricket career started when he went up to Cambridge University, for whom he played for four years. He was captain in 1896 and caused a stir when instructing one of his team to deliberately concede runs to ensure Oxford did not follow on, at a time when the follow-on was compulsory if the team batting second scored 80 or more runs less than the team batting first – the ploy backfired as Oxford went on to win the match.

Mitchell also played for Yorkshire and, by 1898, was selected to play for England. His only two appearances came on England's tour to South Africa in 1898; England won both matches and Mitchell's contribution in the two matches was to score 88 runs, at an average of 22, with a top score of 41.

Mitchell returned to South Africa in 1900 with the Queen's Own Yorkshire Dragoons, fighting in the Second Boer War. Two years later, he was playing cricket for Transvaal, whom he captained to success in the Currie Cup in 1902/03 and 1903/04.

Mitchell stayed on in South Africa and, in 1912, was chosen to captain South Africa in the triangular competition taking place in England between England, Australia and South Africa. Mitchell captained South Africa in one of the matches against England and two of the matches against Australia, all three of which South Africa lost.

Mitchell's last game of first-class cricket was in 1914 when he played for the MCC against Cambridge University. In total he played 199 first-class matches, scoring 9,176 runs at an average of 31.97, with 17 centuries and a top score of 194; he also took 36 wickets at an average of 23.16. His Test match figures were less impressive; in his two games for England, he scored 88 runs at an average of 22 with a top score of 41 and, in his three games for South Africa, he only managed to score 28 runs at an average of 4.66, with a top score of 12.

As well as playing for and captaining Cambridge University at cricket, Mitchell also played for and captained the University side at rugby. Whilst still at university, he was selected to play for England and appeared six times for them, as a forward, in 1895 and 1896. In his fourth international, against Wales, he scored his only try in a 25-0 victory; in his sixth and last international, against Ireland in 1896, he captained the England side to an 11-0 defeat.

Whilst at university, Mitchell also won a blue in athletics for "putting the weight", but not for football, despite subsequently playing in goal for Sussex

After playing his final game of cricket in 1914, Mitchell returned to active duty for the duration of the First World War; after the War, as well as working on the London Stock Exchange, he was also a correspondent for The Cricketer magazine.

Mitchell died in 1935 at the age of 63.

97. Reinhild Moeller (1956-   ), *German Paralympian skier and athlete*

Reinhild Moeller was born in Schwalm-Eder-Krein, in Germany, in 1956. At the age of 3, she lost her left leg in a farm accident.

In 1980, Moeller took part in her first Winter Paralympic Games, winning a bronze medal in the slalom alpine skiing event.

Four years later, she took part in both the Summer Paralympic Games and the Winter Paralympic Games, winning two gold medals in athletics events at the Summer Games and three gold medals and a silver medal in the alpine skiing events at the Winter Games.

In 1988, she again competed at both the Summer Games and the Winter Games, winning a gold and a silver in athletic events at the Summer Games and three gold medals in alpine skiing events at the Winter Games.

Moeller continued to compete in the Winter Paralympic Games from 1990 until 2006. She dominated the alpine skiing events in Tignes in 1990 and in Lillehammer in 1994, winning four golds at each Games – at both Games, she won the gold medal in the Super G, the slalom, the giant slalom and the downhill events. At the 1998 Winter Games, in Nagano, she added two more golds to her tally and, at her last Winter Games in 2006, added a silver, giving her an overall total of 19 gold medals, two silver medals and one bronze medal won in alpine skiing events and three golds and one silver in athletics events.

Moeller moved to the United States in 1990 and is married to the American Paralympic skier Reed Robinson.

98. Heather Moyse (1978-), *Canadian rugby player, bobsleigher and cyclist*

Heather Moyse was born in 1978 on Prince Edward Island, Canada.

Moyse first competed at the Winter Olympics in 2006, when she and her bobsleigh partner Helen Upperton just missed out on a medal, finishing in fourth place. Four years later, with her new partner Kaillie Humphries, she took gold in the bobsleigh event, whilst her former partner Upperton claimed the silver to give Canada first and second places. Four years later, in 2014 in Sochi, Moyse and Humphries retained their title to take the gold for the second time.

Moyse has also competed at three World Championships, in 2008, 2009 and 2011, where she has won two bronze medals with Humphries and at World Cup events since 2005. Her partner until 2008 was Upperton and together they won two gold medals, three silvers and two bronzes; since 2008, she has bobsleighed with Humphries and won four golds, three silvers and two bronzes.

The same year she first competed at the Winter Olympics, Moyse also took part in the Women's Rugby World Cup. Canada came fourth, with Moyse being the top points scorer with 35 points and the top try-scorer with seven tries. At the next Women's Rugby World Cup, four years later in 2010, Canada came sixth, but Moyse was again the leading try-scorer, jointly with New Zealand's Carla Hohepa, with both of them scoring seven tries. In between her appearances at the World Cup, Moyse had taken part in the Hong Kong Sevens and ran in 11 tries in four matches, with Canada finishing runners –up to America. Moyse also represented Canada at the 2013 Rugby Sevens World Cup, Canada again finishing as runners-up.

In 2011, Moyse tried her hand at another sport, cycling. A year later she was competing in the Pan-American Cycling Championships and finished fourth in the time trial event and fifth in the sprint event.

Moyse's other sporting achievements include competing in the Canadian Intercollegiate Athletics Union Championships for four years whilst she was at the University of Waterloo, which she also represented at football (association).

Away from sport, Moyse is an ambassador for the Prince Edward Island potato industry.

99. The Nawab of Pataudi Senior (1910-1952), *English and Indian cricketer and Indian hockey player*

Ifthikar Ali Khan, the 8th Nawab of Pataudi, was born in Delhi in 1910.

Pataudi attended Oxford University from 1927 until 1931 and won cricket blues in 1929, 1930 and 1931. He scored a century in the 1929 Varsity Match but, in the 1931 match scored 238 not out, which remained, until 2005, the highest score in this fixture.

After graduating, Pataudi played cricket for Worcestershire and, at the end of 1932, was picked for the England tour of Australia. He made his debut for England in the first Test, scoring 102 in the first innings. He also played in the second Test, after which he was dropped because he objected to the bodyline tactics employed by the England captain Douglas Jardine to counter the threat of Don Bradman.

Pataudi was picked again for England in 1934 but only played one Test against the touring Australians.

After the Second World War, Pataudi captained India on their three Test tour of England, which England won 1-0 with two matches drawn.

As a Test player, Pataudi was unable to match his performance on his first appearance, finishing with a total of 144 runs for England at an average of 28.80 from his five innings, with just the one century of 102; he fared no better when playing for India, for whom he scored 55 runs at an average of 11, with a top score of 22. His overall record as a first-class cricketer was significantly better; in his 127 first-class matches, he scored a total of 8,750 runs at an average of 48.61, his runs including 29 centuries with his highest score being the 238 not out he scored in the 1931 Varsity Match.

Pataudi also played hockey for India and was selected as a member of the team to compete at the 1928 Olympics in Amsterdam. India won the gold medal, their first of six in succession, without conceding a goal.

Poor health, which Pataudi suffered throughout his career, put an end to his cricket after the tour to England in 1946. He died of a heart attack whilst playing polo, in 1952 at the age of 41. His son, the 9th Nawab of Pataudi, also captained India at cricket, making them the only father and son to have done so.

100. Phil Neville (1977-   ), *English footballer and cricketer*

Phil Neville was born in Bury, Lancashire in 1977.

Neville joined the Manchester United Academy in 1990 and, by the 1994/95 football season, made his debut for Manchester United's first team. Over the next 11 seasons, Neville played, either as a defender or in midfield, 386 games for Manchester United, scoring eight goals for them; during these 11 seasons, Manchester United won the Premier League title six times, the F. A. Cup three times and the UEFA Champions League Cup, including all three in the 1998/99 season.

Neville moved to Everton at the beginning of the 2005/06 season and played his last eight years as a professional footballer with them; during this period he played 303 games for Everton, scoring five goals.

Between 1996 and 2007, Neville won 59 caps playing for England, of which 23 were won coming on as a substitute. His appearances for England included three European Championship Finals, but never a World Cup finals. Before his appearances for the senior team, Neville had captained the England Under-15 team before going on to play for the Under-16, Under-18 and Under-21 teams.

Had Neville not chosen football as a career, he had shown enough promise as a youngster to consider a career in cricket. As well as captaining the England Under-15 team at football, he also captained the England Under-15 cricket team. As a 15 year old, he made an appearance for the Lancashire 2nd XI, making him, at the time, the youngest person to do so. One of his contemporaries at Lancashire was the future England cricket captain Andrew Flintoff but, despite the cricketer Steve Kirby expressing the view that Neville was a better cricketer than Flintoff at that time, Neville opted for football with Manchester United with a salary of £3,000 per week, rather than cricket with Lancashire and a salary of £3,000 per year.

Since retiring from professional football, Neville has worked as a football coach, including with his former club Manchester United; he has also followed the footsteps of his brother Gary into football punditry on television. He has also acquired a stake in Salford City Football Club alongside his former Manchester United teammates Paul Scholes, Ryan Giggs, Nicky Butt and his brother Gary. Neville also works as an ambassador for the charity Bliss, which supports and cares for premature and sick babies.

Neville's brother Gary played 602 games for Manchester United between 1992 and 2011 and 85 games for England between 1995 and 2007 and his twin sister Tracey played 81 international games of netball for England.

101. Isabel Newstead (1955-2007), *Scottish Paralympian swimmer, shot and athlete*

Isabel Newstead (nee Barr) was born in Glasgow in 1955.

At the age of 19, Newstead contracted a flu virus which led to her spinal cord being damaged, which in turn led to her being a tetraplegic. Because she had competed in swimming events before her illness, she continued to swim as part of her rehabilitation.

Newstead first took part in the Paralympic Games in 1980, winning gold in three swimming events, the backstroke, the breaststroke and freestyle over 25 metres. Four years later at the Paralympic Games at Stoke Mandeville, she took part in shooting and track and field events, as well as swimming and came away with three golds, one silver and two bronzes in swimming events, a gold medal in the air pistol shooting event and two bronze medals in field events.

At the 1988 Paralympic games, Newstead's performances were restricted to shooting, in which she won a bronze and track and field, in which she won silver in the shot put event and bronze in the javelin event.

Her fourth and fifth appearances at the Paralympic Games were in 1992, in Barcelona and in 1996, in Atlanta, but brought her no more medals; in 1992, this was partially due to her missing the final of one event following an error by her coach and, in 1996, this was as a result of her breaking a hip in an accident just before the Games' Opening Ceremony. She did however add to her medal tally by winning the gold medal in the air pistol shooting event at both the 2000 Paralympic Games in Sydney and the 2004 Paralympic Games in Athens. Newstead had planned to defend her title and go for a third successive gold in 2008 at Beijing at what would have been her eighth Paralympic Games but she was diagnosed with cancer in 2006 and died a year later at the age of 51.

For her services to disabled sport, Newstead was awarded the MBE in 2001.

102. Chris Nicholson (1967-), *New Zealand speed skater and cyclist*

Chris Nicholson was born in London in 1967.

Nicholson represented New Zealand at the Barcelona Olympics in 1982 in the team time trial cycling event, coming in 10th place. The same year he competed in the Winter Olympics at Albertville in the 1,000 metre speed skating event, in which he was in 17th place and in the 5,000 metre relay, in which the team finished in 4th place, his best Olympic result.

Nicholson was also at the Winter Olympics at Lillehammer two years later, as his country's flag bearer and competing in three speed skating events, the 500 metres, the 1,000 metres and the 5,000 metre relay but was unable to match his performances in Albertville, coming in in 8th place in the 5,000 metre relay, 28th in the 1,000 metres event and 29th in the 500 metres event.

Nicholson's brother, Andrew, also represented New Zealand in speed skating events at the Winter Olympics in 1992, 1994 and 1998.

103. Otto Nothling (1900-1965), *Australian rugby player and cricketer*

Otto Nothling was born in 1900 in Teutoburg (now called Witta), in Queensland.

Nothling played full-back at rugby in 19 matches for Australia between 1921 and 1924, his first international being when he was only 20 years old. Ten of the matches he played in were against New Zealand, six against the New Zealand Maoris and three against South Africa; of his 19 matches, in which he scored 36 points consisting of one try, five conversions, five penalties and two drop goals, eight were won and 11 lost – four of his eight wins were against New Zealand and four against the Maoris.

Four years after he was last selected to play rugby for Australia, Nothling was selected to play cricket for them against the touring English team, in the Second Test of the 1928/29 series; 12th man for Australia in this Test was Don Bradman. Australia batted first and Nothling was bowled by Harold Larwood for 8; Nothling then opened the bowling for Australia and, although he did not pick up a wicket in his 42 overs in England's innings of 636, he was Australia's most economical bowler conceding only 60 runs. Nothling also opened the bowling in England's second innings, but he only bowled four overs, for 12 runs, before England reached their target of 16 runs to win the match by eight wickets.

Nothling was not picked again to play for Australia but he can at least claim that, in his one Test, he was selected ahead of the great Don Bradman, who was, in this Test, 12th man for the only time in his career after having been dropped.

Nothling played a total of 21 games of first-class cricket. He played for New South Wales for three seasons and then played for two seasons for Queensland as his medical practice was based in Brisbane. In his 21 games, he scored 882 runs at an average of 24.50, with one century to his name, a score of 121 and took 36 wickets at an average of 41.05.

Nothling attended Sydney University where, as well as representing the university at cricket and rugby, he also excelled in track events, breaking javelin-throwing and shot-putting records.

After his sporting days were over, Nothling became a prominent dermatologist. In the Second World War, Nothling served with the Australian Army Medical Corps in the Middle East and Greece before poor health led to him being sent back to Australia, where he continued with his medical practice, until his death in 1965 at the age of 65.

104. Charlie Oliver (1905-1977), *New Zealand rugby player and cricketer*

Charlie Oliver was born in Wanganui, New Zealand, in 1905.

Oliver was a right-hand batsman who made his cricket debut for Canterbury in 1924; a year later, he was picked to play for New Zealand on their tour to Australia in 1925/26, playing in their matches against Queensland, Victoria, South Australia and New South Wales. In 1927, he toured with the New Zealand team to England and played in ten of their matches. As with the earlier tour to Australia, none of the matches were Test matches as it was not until 1930 that New Zealand was awarded Test status.

Oliver played a total of 16 games for New Zealand, in which he scored 441 runs at an average of 18.37, with a highest score of 68. He played his last game of first-class cricket in 1943; in his 35 games of first-class cricket, he scored a total of 1,301 runs at an average of 23.23, with a top score of 91.

Oliver also played rugby for Canterbury as a centre. He was part of the New Zealand team which toured Australia in 1929 and played in both Tests, which New Zealand lost; Oliver did however manage to score a try in the first Test.

Oliver next played for New Zealand when they played Australia in 1934; again Oliver ended up on the losing side. A year later, he was part of the All Black team which toured the British Isles. He played in the four matches against Scotland, Ireland, Wales and England. New Zealand won the matches against Scotland and Ireland, with Oliver scoring his second Test try against Ireland but both Wales and England got the better of the tourists, Wales winning narrowly by 13-12 and England winning 13-0, with Prince Alexander Obolensky scoring two tries for England on his debut.

Altogether, Oliver played 33 games of rugby for New Zealand, winning 26 of them, drawing one and losing six. He captained them on nine occasions, seven in matches on the tour to the British Isles and two against Canadian teams on the way back to New Zealand, but never in a Test match. In addition to his two tries in Tests, he scored 14 tries and kicked eight conversions and one penalty for New Zealand, giving him a total of 67 points.

In later life, Oliver moved to Australia and died at the age of 71 in 1977.

105. Tuppy Owen-Smith (1909-1990), *South African cricketer and English rugby player*

Harold Geoffrey Owen-Smith, known as "Tuppy", was born in Cape Town on 1909.

He first played cricket for Western Province in the 1927/28 season and was picked for the South African tour to England in 1929, when he played in all five Tests in a series won by England 2-0, with three Tests drawn. Owen-Smith was a right-handed batsman who scored 252 runs in the series, at an average of 42, with a top score of 129, his only Test century. As a bowler he had less success, taking no wickets in his 26 overs and conceding 113 runs. He was however a fine fielder, as highly regarded as his compatriot Colin Bland and the West Indian Clive Lloyd were in the 1960s and 1970s.

Although Owen-Smith was not picked to play cricket for South Africa again, he continued to play cricket, first for Oxford University for three years whilst on a Rhodes Scholarship and then for Middlesex when qualifying as a physician whilst at St Mary's Hospital, before returning to South Africa and playing for Western Province until the 1949/50 season. During a first-class career in which he played 101 games, he scored 4,059 runs at an average of 26.88, with three centuries to his name and a highest score of 168; he also took 319 wickets with his leg breaks, at an average of 23.22.

Whilst at Oxford, Owen-Smith also represented the University in athletics, boxing (having been a champion lightweight boxer) and rugby. In 1934, a year after leaving Oxford, he was picked to play rugby for England at full-back and played in all three of England's matches as they won The Triple Crown. He did not appear again for England until 1936 but played in four matches that year, including in the famous 13-0 victory over New Zealand in which Charlie Oliver (see Chapter 104) was playing. When England played Wales and Ireland later that year, they were unable to match their performance against New Zealand, the game against Wales being drawn and the game against Ireland being lost, but a year later, with Owen-Smith as captain, England repeated their Triple Crown success with a 4-3 win over Wales, a 9-8 win over Ireland and a 6-3 win over Scotland – the 4-3 win over Wales was due to England kicking a drop goal, which was then worth four points and Wales failing to convert their try, which was only worth three points. In the 10 rugby internationals in which Owen-Smith played for England, although he did not score any points, England won eight of them, drew one of them and only lost once.

On his return to South Africa in 1938, as well as continuing to play cricket, Owen-Smith carried on with his medical practice.

Owen-Smith died in 1990 at the age of 81. Although his Test career was a relatively short one, his cricket aroused enthusiasm, to such an extent that he was likened to Denis Compton (see Chapter 25); in the words of Wisden 1991, "quite apart from the exhilarating nature of his play, it was the young man himself who had such a wide appeal...... like Compton, he communicated his enjoyment of cricket to thousands". And, like Compton, he excelled not just at cricket.

106. Curly Page (1902-1987), *New Zealand rugby player and cricketer*

Milford Laurenson Page, better known as Curly Page, was born in Christchurch, New Zealand in 1902.

In 1928, Page played scrum-half for New Zealand against New South Wales in a match narrowly won by the All Blacks, 11-8. This was his only appearance for New Zealand as a rugby player as he wanted to concentrate more on his cricket, having first played cricket for Canterbury in 1921 whilst still at school.

A year before he played for the All Blacks and before New Zealand had been awarded Test status, Page had been on a New Zealand cricket tour to England. By the time England toured New Zealand in 1929/30, New Zealand had been awarded Test status; the tour included New Zealand's first four Tests and Page played in all of them, the series being won by England 1-0, with three matches drawn. 18 months later New Zealand toured England again, playing three Tests in a series won 1-0 by England; again, Page played in all three Tests, including the one at Lord's where he scored his only Test century, an innings of 104, earning him a place on the honours board.

The following winter South Africa toured New Zealand for their first series against each other, with Page now captaining New Zealand in a series which they lost 2-0. A year later, it was the turn of England to tour again; Page was still captain and both Tests in the series were drawn.

New Zealand did not play another Test until their tour to England in 1937. Page was still captain but New Zealand failed to record their first success in Tests, going down 1-0 in a three Test series.

By the time the Second World War had broken out, New Zealand had played 14 Tests, of which five had been lost and nine drawn and Page was the only New Zealander to have played in all of them. In his 14 Tests, Page had scored 492 runs at an average of 24.60, with his only century being the one he scored at Lord's in 1931. His rarely-used bowling had brought him five wickets at an average of 46.20.

Over a first-class career from 1921 until 1937, Page played in 132 matches, scoring 5,837 runs at an average of 29.88. He scored nine centuries with a highest score of 206 and took 73 wickets at an average of 32.38, with best bowling figures of four for 10.

Page died in 1987 at the age of 84.

107. James Cecil Parke (1881-1946), *Irish rugby player and tennis player*

James Cecil Parke was born in County Monaghan in 1881.

Between 1901 and 1908, Parke played rugby for Leinster 10 times but between 1903 and 1909 made twice as many appearances for Ireland as he did for Leinster. Between 1906 and 1909, he did not miss any of

Ireland's games against the other Home Nations or the fixture against France in 1909 when they joined the Five Nations Championships. His overall record in his 20 internationals was six wins and 14 defeats, with him scoring 36 points playing at centre, his points being made up of two tries, six conversions, five penalties and a goal scored from a mark; scoring a goal from a mark was rare and, following changes in the laws of rugby in 1977, points could not be scored from a mark.

In 1906, Parke played golf for Ireland and two years later competed at the Olympic Games at tennis, winning the silver medal in the men's doubles. 1912 was however his most successful year on the tennis court, with him winning the men's singles and the men's doubles at what was then called the Australasian Championships and is one of the four major tennis tournaments along with the French Championships, Wimbledon and the US Open. As home rule for Ireland had not yet been implemented, he qualified to play for Great Britain and was a member of the team which won the Davis Cup that year; he played in two of the singles matches, winning them both and the doubles match, which Great Britain lost, in a 3-2 victory over Australia, with Parke winning the deciding rubber. By the end of the year, he was ranked three in the world. A year later, Parke again represented Great Britain in the Davis Cup final which was won by the USA, despite Parke winning his two singles matches.

In 1914, Parke won another major title at tennis, the mixed doubles at Wimbledon with Ethel Larcombe; in the final, they beat the New Zealander Anthony Wilding and his French partner Marguerite Broquedin – it proved to be Wilding's last competitive match as he was killed on the Western Front in 1915.

Parkes, like Wilding, served in the Great War, first with the Leinster Regiment and, after being wounded in Gallipoli in 1915, with the Essex Regiment.

After the War though and despite having been wounded, Parke was able to continue with his tennis, reaching the men's doubles final at Wimbledon in 1920, with Algernon Kingsgate, before losing to the Americans Chuck

Garland and Norris Williams. His ranking that year was four in the world, at the age of 39.

As well as representing Ireland at golf and rugby and Great Britain at tennis, Parke also represented Ireland at athletics and was an excellent cricketer.

Parke died in 1946 at the age of 64. In 2009, 100 years after his last appearance for Ireland at rugby, The Daily Telegraph described Parke as Ireland's finest ever sportsman.

108. Tony Pawson (1921-2012), *English cricketer, footballer and angler*

Tony Pawson was born in Chertsey, Surrey in 1921.

Pawson first made a name for himself as a cricketer at the age of 15 when, in a match for the public schools under-16 team, he scored 237 at Lord's; at the time, this was the highest score by anyone at Lord's under the age of 18.

The Second World War, during which Pawson served with the Rifle Brigade in Italy and North Africa, delayed his first-class career until 1946, when he played his first game for Kent. That same year Pawson went up to Oxford University and the following summer scored 103 on his debut for them against Gloucestershire. The following year, in 1948, he captained the Oxford team, following in the footsteps of his father, who had captained the side in 1910.

As well as playing for Oxford University and Kent, Pawson also played for the MCC alongside Denis Compton (see Chapter 25) against the touring South Africans in 1947. By the time he retired in 1953, Pawson had played a total of 69 first-class matches, scoring 3,807 runs at an average of 37.32; his seven centuries included a highest score of 150 and one of his centuries was the 135 which he scored in the Varsity Match against Cambridge in 1947.

Pawson also played football for Oxford University and, after playing for the England amateur team in 1948, was picked as a member of the Great Britain Olympic team that year; however, he was not picked to play in any of their games. He did play though two games for Charlton Athletic, the first on Christmas Day in 1951 against Tottenham Hotspur when, after trailing 2-0, he scored the winner in a 3-2 win when he drove home a clearance by the future World Cup winning manager Alf Ramsay. He also played football for the amateur club Pegasus and was a member of their Amateur Cup winning teams of 1951 and 1953.

Pawson's commitment to cricket was restricted by his commitment to angling; when being told by the Kent captain in 1946 after receiving his cap that he was in for the season, he replied "Sorry, skipper, I am off fishing". Pawson began fishing as a child on the Nile, when his father was posted to work for the Sudan Civil Service. In 1982, he was a member of the English fly-fishing team that won the World Championships and two years later, he became the first Briton to win an individual World Championship title.

As well as spending time fishing, Pawson also became the personnel director of Reed International, a position he combined with being a cricket and football correspondent for The Observer newspaper. In 1988, Pawson was awarded an OBE for services to angling.

Pawson died in 2012 at the age of 91.

109. Cato Zahl Pedersen (1959-   ), *Norwegian Paralympian athlete and skier*

Cato Zahl Pedersen was born in Norway in 1959; whilst a child, he lost both his arms in an accident.

In 1980 and 1984, Pedersen took part in both the Summer Paralympic Games and the Winter Paralympic Games, competing in field and track events at the Summer Games and in alpine and cross-country skiing events at the Winter Games. He won six gold medals as an athlete at the Summer Games.

Pedersen continued to compete in the Winter Paralympic Games in 1988 and 1994 but only in the alpine skiing events. In addition to the six gold medals he won as an athlete at the Summer Games, he won seven golds at the Winter Games, six in alpine skiing events and one at cross-country skiing.

At the end of 1994, Pedersen was part of a four-man team which skied to the South Pole, carrying his sledge with a prosthetic right arm.

Pedersen returned to the Paralympics in 2000 when he took part in the sailing events, but was unable to add to his overall tally of 13 gold medals and one silver medal he had already won.

110. Nova Peris (1971-), *Australian athlete and hockey player*

Nova Peris was born in Darwin, Australia in 1971.

In 1996, Peris became the first Aboriginal Australian to win a gold medal at the Olympics when she was a member of the team that won the hockey event. Her success at the Olympics followed on from the success she had enjoyed as a member of the Australian women's hockey team which had won the Champions Trophy in 1993 and 1995 and the World Cup in 1994.

In 1997, Peris decided to concentrate on athletics. She competed at the Commonwealth Games in 1998, winning the gold medal in the 200 metres event and in the 4 x 100 metres relay event. A year later, she ran in the 200 metres event at the World Athletics Championships and, in 2000, ran in the 400 metres event and the 4 x 400 metres relay event at the Sydney Olympics, reaching the semi-finals in the individual event and coming fifth in the relay event.

After retiring from athletics, Peris entered the world of politics, after being invited by the Australian Prime Minister to join the Labor Party. In 2013, she became the first female Aborigine to be elected to the federal parliament.

111. Ellyse Perry (1990-   ), *Australian footballer and cricketer*

Ellyse Perry was born in Wahroonga, New South Wales in 1990.

In July 2007, at the age of 16, Perry played her first game of cricket for Australia, a one day international against New Zealand; less than two weeks later, she played her first game of football for Australia, an Olympic qualifying match against Hong Kong, a game in which she scored after only two minutes.

Since her first appearance for Australia on the cricket pitch, Perry has played in the Women's World Cup in 2009 and 2013 and the Women's Twenty20 World Cup in 2010, 2012 and 2014. In the Women's World Cup, she was on the winning side in 2013, taking three for 19 in the final against the West Indies and, in the Women's Twenty20 World Cup, she was on the winning side in 2010 against New Zealand and in 2012 and 2014, both times against England; in the 2010 final, she was awarded the player of the final for her three wickets for 18 runs as Australia won by three runs and, in the 2014 final, she took two wickets for 13 runs in her 4 overs.

With women playing relatively few Test matches, Perry had only played five Tests for Australia prior to Australia's Ashes tour to England in July 2015; in these five Tests, she has scored 210 runs at an average of 40.20 and with a top score of 71 and taken 18 wickets at an average 20.27, with best figures in an innings of five for 38. In one day internationals up to July 2015, she has played in 64 matches for Australia, scoring 973 runs at an average of 36.03 and with a top score of 90 not out and taking 89 wickets at an average of 24.01 and with best bowling figures of five for 19. She had also played in 63 Twenty20 internationals for Australia prior to the 2015 Ashes tour, scoring 331 runs at an average of 19.47 with a top score of 41 not out and taking 62 wickets at an average of 19.59, with best figures of four for 20. With a lower bowling average than batting average in Tests and ODIs, she is currently one of the best all-rounders in cricket.

Perry's cricket commitments have made it increasingly difficult for her to combine her cricket with her football. Her football club Canberra United wanted her to commit full-time to football, something which, as she was unwilling to do, saw her move to Sydney FC. However, her commitment to cricket has seen her omitted from recent teams selected to represent Australia at football competitions, but not before she had played for them 18 times and scored four goals. Also, her cricket did not prevent her from participating in the FIFA Women's World Cup in 2011. Perry played in Australia's 2-1 win over Norway and also when Australia lost 3-1 in the quarter-finals to Sweden - Perry scored Australia's goal, one which is considered by many to be the best goal ever scored by an Australian, male or female, at the World Cup finals.

Opportunities for her football on an international stage may be threatened by her cricket and by the reluctance of some managers to pick players who cannot commit full-time to football but she still has many years of cricket ahead of her; her performances in England in 2014 when, despite being on the losing side, she was named as player of the Ashes series against England, suggest that she is going to be a thorn in England's side for many years to come.

112. Fred Perry (1909-1995), *English tennis player and table tennis player*

Fred Perry was born in Stockport, Greater Manchester in 1909.

Although Perry is best known for his achievements on the tennis court and the Fred Perry label on sports clothing is instantly recognisable, Perry was a world champion table tennis player before he had won the first of his eight singles titles at any of the four "major" events.

Perry took part in the Table Tennis World Championships in both 1928 and 1929. At the 1928 Championships, he won the silver medal in the doubles and the bronze medal in both the mixed doubles and the team event. A year later, he became world champion when he won the gold medal, to add to the bronze medals he won in the doubles and in the team event.

The first year Perry entered the singles at Wimbledon was the same year he was the table tennis world champion, but it was not until 1933 that he won his first major singles title, the US Open. In 1934, he won his only Australian title and his first Wimbledon title, as well as retaining his US title and, when in 1935 he won his only French title, he became the first man to win all four major singles titles. He retained his Wimbledon title in 1935 and, in 1936, won his third successive Wimbledon title and his third US title, before turning professional. When winning his third Wimbledon title, he took only 40 minutes to beat the German Gottfried von Cramm, who was suffering with a groin strain, 6-1, 6-1, 6-0 – this compares with the 3 hours 9 minutes which it took the next British man, Andy Murray, to win Wimbledon when beating Novak Djokovic in straight sets in 2013.

As well as winning eight singles titles at the majors, Perry also won the French doubles title in 1933 and the Australian doubles title in 1934, both with his compatriot Pat Hughes and the mixed doubles title at the French Championships in 1932 with compatriot Betty Nuthall, the mixed doubles title at the US in 1932 with American Sarah Cooke and the mixed doubles title at Wimbledon in 1935 and 1936 with the American Dorothy Round.

Perry was also a member of the Great Britain team which won the Davis Cup four years in a row from 1933 to 1936; in all his Davis Cup appearances, Perry won 34 of his 38 singles matches and 11 of his 14 doubles matches.

After winning the US title in 1936, Perry turned professional, thereby making himself ineligible to compete at the major events. He did play numerous exhibition matches, most of which were against the American Ellworth Vines (see Chapter 158) and, after he turned professional after winning all four majors in 1938, the American Don Budge. Perry also competed in the US Pro tournament, the only major tournament for professionals at the time, from 1938 to 1941, winning the title in 1938 and 1941 and being runner-up in 1939 and 1940.

Although Perry continued competing in tournaments for professionals into the 1950s, he had, in 1952, launched the first Fred Perry tennis shirt and Fred Perry sportswear has been a successful brand ever since. 1952 was also the year he married his fourth wife, whom he remained married to until his death in 1995 at the age of 85.

Perry's success as a tennis player resulted in a number of memorials to him, perhaps the best known being the bronze statue of him unveiled in 1984 at The All England Club where the Wimbledon Championships are held. However, his success on tennis courts around the world has over-shadowed his performances at table tennis, the first sport at which he proved himself to be world class.

Author's Note. To many, it may seem that the skills required to be a top class table tennis player and a top class tennis player are similar; however, in his book Bounce, the international table tennis player Matthew Syed recounts the time he pitted his skills against the former Wimbledon champion Michael Stich. Syed was renowned for his quick reactions and wanted to test them against the big serve of Stich. Syed faced four serves from Stich and was not able to get his racket to the ball for any of them. A skilful table tennis player does therefore not necessarily have what is required to be a star at tennis.

113. Liz Perry (1987-   ), *New Zealand cricketer and hockey player*

Liz Perry was born in Taumarunui, New Zealand in 1987.

Perry played cricket for New Zealand between 2010 and 2012, as a right-hand bat and right-arm medium pace bowler; she played for her country in eight one day internationals and 25 Twenty20 matches. In her eight ODIs, Perry scored 159 runs at an average of 22.71 with a highest score of

70 and, in her Twenty20 internationals, scored 313 runs at an average of 18.41 with a highest score of 50 not out.

Perry also played hockey for New Zealand, having played for the Canterbury Cats in the New Zealand Hockey League.

Since playing international cricket and hockey, Perry has been carrying out research at the University of Canterbury, investigating and examining the experiences of Australian and New Zealand women who have played cricket in England and how they adapt to sport and life away from home; whilst carrying out her research, Perry also played cricket for Yorkshire.

114. Vic Pollard (1945-   ), *New Zealand cricketer and footballer*

Victor Pollard was born in Burnley in 1945 and emigrated to New Zealand in 1952.

Pollard was a right-handed batsman and right-arm off-break bowler who was selected to tour with the New Zealand team to India and Pakistan in 1965 after just six games of first-class cricket. He continued to play for New Zealand up until 1973, his last Test appearances being on the tour that year to England, where he enjoyed enormous success, averaging 100.66 with the bat in the three Tests.

At club level, Pollard first played for Central Districts before moving to Canterbury; due to his reluctance to play on Sundays because of his religious beliefs, which led to him missing a number of games, Pollard lost the Canterbury captaincy and, with it, any realistic chance to captain the national team.

Pollard retired from Test cricket after the tour to England, having played in 32 Tests, scoring 1,266 runs at an average of 24.34, with two centuries and a highest score of 116 and taking 40 wickets at an average of 46.32 with best figures of three for 3. Pollard retired from first-class cricket 18 months later, having played 130 games of first-class cricket and scoring 5,314 runs at an average of 30.54, with six centuries and a top score of 146 and taking 224 wickets at an average of 30.94 with best figures of seven for 65.

Pollard was also a footballer and played in seven internationals for New Zealand between 1968 and 1972.

After retiring from cricket, Pollard became a teacher.

115. Albert Powell (1873-1948), *South African cricketer and rugby player*

Albert "Bertie" Powell was born in Kimberley, South Africa in 1873.

Powell was a right-hand batsman and right-arm bowler who started playing cricket for Griqualand West in 1892; in 1899, he was selected to play for South Africa in the second Test against the touring England team. Despite South Africa having a first innings lead of 85, England won the match by 210 runs after dismissing South Africa in their second innings for just 35; Powell scored only 5 runs in the first innings but top-scored with 11 in the second innings; in England's second innings, he bowled four overs, taking one wicket for 10 runs, but it was not enough for the selectors to pick him again.

Powell continued to turn out occasionally for Griqualand West until 1905 and, by the time he retired, he had played 16 first-class games of cricket, in which he scored 296 runs with a top score of 31 and an average of 9.86; his bowling had brought him 12 wickets at an average of 34.33.

Prior to his selection for the South African cricket team, Powell had been picked to play centre at rugby for South Africa against the team visiting from Great Britain in 1896. As with his cricket, Powell was only selected on the one occasion for the national rugby team, a closely-fought match which Great Britain won 9-3.

Powell died in 1948 at the age of 75.

116. Cotah Ramaswami (1896-?), *Indian cricketer and tennis player*

Cotah Ramaswami was born in Madras in 1896.

Ramaswami attended Cambridge University from 1919 until 1923, winning a blue in tennis. In 1922, whilst still a student, he was picked to play in the Davis Cup for India and played in the doubles matches in their win over Romania and their subsequent defeat by Spain. Partnering Dr Fayzee, Ramaswami won both his matches – the doubles win over Spain was against the Spanish pairing of Comte de Gomar and Flaquer, whom a year later were the runners-up in the men's doubles at Wimbledon. 1922 also saw Ramaswami playing at Wimbledon, where he reached the second round in the men's singles.

After graduating, Ramaswami returned to live in India where he played first-class cricket, batting left-handed and bowling right-arm. At the age of 40, he was selected for the tour of India to England and played in the second and third Tests; he was not selected again but, in his first Test, which was drawn, he scored 40 and 60 and, in his second Test, which England won by nine wickets, he scored 29 and 41 not out, giving him a Test average of 56.66.

Ramaswami played a total of 53 first-class games of cricket, in which he scored 2,400 runs at an average of 28.91, with two centuries and a top score of 127 not out; he also took 30 wickets at an average of 33.06.

After retiring from cricket, he became a national selector and managed the Indians on their tour to the West Indies in 1952/53.

Ramaswami had two brothers, a son and four nephews who also played first-class cricket. In 1985, Ramaswami left his home, never to return. It is not known when he died but CricketArchive and Wisden both suggest that it was in January 1990.

Ramaswami is one of only three Indian Test cricketers who have represented India in two sports, the other two being M. J. Gopalan (see Chapter

53) and The Nawab of Pataudi Senior (see Chapter 99); a fourth, Syed Mohammed Hadi (1899-1971), represented India at tennis playing in the Davis Cup in 1924 and 1925 and at the Olympics in 1924 and at cricket, in an unofficial Test and on tour to England in 1936 but he never played Test cricket for India.

117. Jonty Rhodes (1969 -), *South African cricketer and hockey player*

Jonathan Neil Rhodes, better known as Jonty Rhodes, was born in Pietermaritzburg in 1969.

Rhodes was a right-handed batsman who played his first game of first-class cricket in 1988 and, by 1992, he was making his debut for South Africa, both in Tests and one-day internationals.

His Test career lasted until 2000 when he retired from Test cricket to concentrate on one-day cricket. In his 52 Tests, Rhodes scored 2,532 runs at an average of 35.66, with three centuries to his name and a top score of 117. His one-day career continued until 2003, by which time he had played in 245 ODIs for South Africa, scoring 5,935 runs at an average of 35.11, with two centuries and a top score of 121. That he played less games of first-class cricket than international ODIs is a reflection of the growing popularity of limited overs cricket during his playing days – by the time he retired from first-class cricket, he had played only 164 games, scoring 9,546 runs at an average of 41.14, with 22 centuries to his name and a highest score of 172.

As a cricketer, Rhodes is perhaps best remembered for his fielding; the number of runs he saved is not recorded but on many an occasion batsmen found themselves denied what they thought were certain boundaries, whilst others found themselves heading back to the pavilion after a spectacular catch or run out. Although Rhodes only took 34 catches in Tests and 105 in ODIs, he still holds the world record for the most catches in an ODI other than by a wicketkeeper, the five he took in a game against the West Indies in 1993 - one of his victims was Brian Lara, who could hardly believe the catch Rhodes had taken to dismiss him; his run out of Pakistan's Inzaman-ul-Haq in the 1992 World Cup was one of the highlights of that World Cup.

In the same year Rhodes was making his debut for South Africa at cricket, he was also playing centre-forward at hockey for South Africa in their qualifying games for the Olympics in Barcelona. South Africa failed to qualify for the Barcelona Olympics but, four years later, when the team did qualify for the 1996 Olympics, Rhodes was unable to join the team because of a hamstring injury.

Since retiring from cricket, Rhodes has worked with a number of cricket teams as a fielding coach, as well as working an account executive for an international bank; he is employed as an ambassador for South African tourism.

118. Alfred Richards (1867-1904), *South African cricketer and rugby player*

Alfred Richards was born in Grahamstown, South Africa in 1867.

In 1891, Richards represented South Africa at rugby playing in the position of inside-centre and fly-half. He played in all three matches against the touring British Isles team, captaining South Africa in the last match of the series, which was won by the British Isles 3-0.

After this series, Richards did not play rugby again. He did however continue to play cricket and, in 1894, scored 108 for Western Province against Natal, to win the Currie Cup. His next game of cricket was against the team touring from England in 1894/95, captained by Lord Hawke. After scoring 58 out of a total of 122, Richards was selected to play in the third representative match against Lord Hawke's team, which the tourists won by an innings and 33 runs, with Richards scoring 6 and 0 for the South African team. Richards did not play cricket again after this match but, as he was playing for a representative South African team, the match was retrospectively granted Test match status. In total, Richards played only nine games of first-class cricket, scoring 346 runs at an average of 23.06, his only century being the 108 he scored against Natal.

Richards died in Rhodesia in 1904 at the age of 36. His brother Dicky also played Test cricket for South Africa, but was less successful than Alfred – he played in only one Test, scoring 0 in a first innings total of 47 and 4 in a second innings total of 43, in a match England won by an innings and 202 runs.

119. Viv Richards (1952-), *West Indian cricketer and Antiguan footballer*

Sir Isaac Vivian Alexander Richards was born in St Johns, Antigua in 1952.

Richards played his first game of first-class cricket in 1971 and, by the time he retired in 1993, he had proved himself to be one of the greatest batsmen of all time. During the early part of his career, he also played football for Antigua and Barbuda in their World Cup qualifying matches, making him the only man to have played both World Cup cricket and World Cup football.

Richards played his first Test match for the West Indies in 1974 and a year later was playing for them in the inaugural cricket World Cup, a 60 over competition won by the West Indies; although Richards had little success with the bat in the final, he was responsible for the running out of three of the Australian batsmen. Four years later, at the second World Cup, Richards was again on the winning side, picking up the man-of-the-match award in the final after scoring a magnificent 138 not out against England.

Richards captained the West Indies in 50 of the 121 Tests he played; he scored a total of 8,540 Test runs, at an average of 50.23, scoring 24 centuries with a top score of 291; his century against England on his home ground in Antigua in 1986 took merely 56 balls and was, until Pakistan's Misbak-ul-Haq equalled it playing against New Zealand in 2014, the fastest century in terms of balls received. His off-spin bowling, which with the pace attack the West Indies had was rarely needed, brought him 32 wickets at an average of 61.37 and he held 122 catches.

Richards' batting style was particularly well suited to one day cricket and he played 187 ODIs for the West Indies, scoring 6,721 runs at an average of 47; his 11 ODI centuries include an innings of 189 not out against England in 1984, an innings rated by Wisden in 2002 as the greatest one day innings of all time – his 10th wicket unbroken partnership with Michael Holding saw them put on 106 runs for the last wicket, with Holding's contribution being 12 of these runs. He also took 118 wickets with his bowling in ODIs, with a best bowling analysis of six for 41 and took 110 catches.

In addition to playing for the West Indies, Richards played for the Combined Islands, the Leeward Islands, Somerset, Glamorgan and Queensland; in all first-class cricket, he played 507 games, scoring 36,212 runs at an average of 49.40, with 114 centuries and a highest score of 322; he ended up taking 223 wickets bowling, at an average of 45.15 and taking 464 catches.

As well as having been chosen as playing the greatest ODI international innings, Richards was voted in 2002 as being the greatest one day batsman of all time and the third greatest batsman of all time, behind Don Bradman and Sachin Tendulkar. He was also voted by an electorate of 100 chosen by Wisden to have been one of the greatest five cricketers of the 20th century, along with Don Bradman, Gary Sobers, Jack Hobbs and Shane Warne.

It is hardly surprising that Richards was unable to match on the football field the success he enjoyed with the bat and ball. Picked for Antigua and Barbuda's qualifying matches for the 1974 World Cup, Richards played two matches against Trinidad and Tobago and two against Surinam; all four matches were lost, with Antigua and Barbuda scoring three goals whilst conceding 22. At least they had the consolation of knowing that England also failed to qualify for the World Cup finals that year.

Although he retired from playing cricket more than 20 years ago, Richards' reputation as a cricketer is such that his views on the game are always in demand and his services as a commentator frequently sought.

In 1994, Richards was awarded the OBE for services to cricket and, in 1999, the Antiguan government bestowed him a knighthood.

120. V. Y. Richardson (1894-1969), *Australian cricketer, baseball player, tennis player, golfer and Australian Rules footballer*

Victor York Richardson was born in Adelaide, South Australia in 1894.

Richardson made his debut in first-class cricket in 1919 and, by 1924, had been picked to represent Australia. He played a total of 19 Test matches for Australia and captained them on their five Test tour to South Africa in 1935/36. Two years earlier, he had been vice-captain during the infamous Bodyline series, during which he remarked to his teammates "Which of you bastards called Larwood a bastard instead of this bastard?", the "this bastard" being the unpopular Douglas Jardine.

Richardson scored a total of 706 runs in his 19 Tests between 1924 and 1935, at an average of 25.53, with one century, a score of 138 against England in 1925. In all his 184 first-class matches, he scored 10,727 runs at an average of 37.63, with 27 centuries and a top score of 231. As well as being a useful batsman, Richardson was an outstanding fielder and, during his playing days, was rated the best fielder of his time.

Before Richardson had made his first-class cricket debut, he had already represented Sturt Football Club at Australian Rules football in the South Australia National football league; he played 114 games for them from 1915 until his retirement in 1927, captaining them for three seasons; during this period, he also represented South Australia 10 times at Australian Rules football. In 1920, for his performances as captain and coach of

Sturt, Richardson won the Magarey Medal, the South Australian Football League's highest individual award.

Richardson also represented South Australia at golf and Australia at baseball and was the South Australian tennis champion.

Although he did not play them to a representative level, Richardson also excelled at basketball, lacrosse and swimming.

After retiring from cricket, Richardson worked as a radio commentator, forming a much-liked partnership with the English cricketer Arthur Gilligan.

Richardson was awarded the OBE in 1954 for services to cricket; he died in 1969 at the age of 75. Two of his grandsons, Ian and Graham Chappell, followed in his footsteps, also captaining Australia at cricket; a third grandson, Trevor Chappell, also played cricket for Australia but is perhaps best remembered for the "grubber" he bowled to Brian McKechnie (see Chapter 90), to make it virtually impossible for a winning six to be hit off the last ball of a match against New Zealand in 1981.

121. Walter Robins (1906-1968), *English cricketer and footballer*

Walter Robins was born in Stafford in 1906.

In 1925, whilst still at Highgate School, Robins played his first game of cricket for Middlesex. A year later, he was playing for Cambridge University and, a year after graduating, playing for England. Over the next 14 years, he played in 19 Tests for England, captaining them in the three Test series against New Zealand in 1937.

The previous year, Robins had been vice-captain on the tour to Australia. In the third Test with England two-nil up in the series, Robins dropped Bradman early in his innings which Bradman took full advantage of, going on to score 270 – Australia won the Test and went on to win the series

3-2 and retain the Ashes. After apologising to his captain Gubby Allen for dropping the catch, Allen responded "Don't give it a thought Walter, you've probably cost us the Ashes, but don't give it a thought"; this was not entirely fair as it occurred when Australia were already 200 ahead in their second innings. Robins did at least have the consolation of knowing that he had got the better of Bradman six years earlier when he bowled Bradman with a googly, which Bradman did not read and to which he offered no stroke.

In his 19 Tests, Robins proved to be a useful all-rounder, scoring 612 runs at an average of 26.60, with one century, a score of 108, to his name and taking, with his leg-breaks, 64 wickets at an average of 27.46, with best bowling figures of six for 32. His first-class career ended in 1950 by which time he had played 379 matches, in which he scored 13,884 runs at an average of 26.39, with 11 centuries and a highest score of 140 and taken 969 wickets at an average of 23.30.

Robins was also a useful footballer. As with his cricket, he played in three Varsity matches for Cambridge against Oxford, playing in the position of right-wing. He also played for the leading amateur club, Corinthians and was twice picked to play for Nottingham Forest, who were then playing in the Second Division, the equivalent of what is now the Championship League division. His first game for them was the home fixture on Christmas Day 1929 against Barnsley, who they beat 4-0; he was not selected for the league fixture the next day, away against Barnsley or the league fixture two days after that against Chelsea but played his second game for Nottingham Forest exactly a year later, this time the Christmas Day fixture against Reading, which they drew 1-1.

After retiring from cricket, Robins became a selector and managed England's tour to the West Indies in 1959/60. He died in 1968 at the age of 62.

122. Rebecca Rolls (1975-), *New Zealand cricketer and footballer*

Rebecca Rolls was born in Napier, New Zealand in 1975.

With Women's Test matches being infrequent, Rolls had limited opportunities to prove herself other than in limited overs cricket but, in the one Test she has played, against England in 2004, she scored 71 in her only innings, giving her an enviable average of 71. In limited overs cricket, she first played in a one day international for New Zealand in 1997 and, by the time she played her last ODI in 2007, she had played in 104 ODIs and, in doing so, became the second female New Zealander to play in one hundred ODIs; included in the ODIs she played in are those when New Zealand won the Women's World Cup in 2000.

With the bat in her ODIs, Rolls has scored 2,201 runs at an average of 25.01 and made two centuries, with a top score of 114; she also kept wicket for the New Zealand team and her 133 dismissals, made up of 89 catches and 44 stumpings, are the highest of any female in ODIs.

Rolls also kept goal at football and made her debut for New Zealand in 1994; by 1996, she had played 11 times for New Zealand but did not play again for them until 16 years later when she was recalled to the team, for the 2012 Cyprus Cup. That year she was also included in the squad of 18 for the London Olympics and a year later played in the final of the Valais Cup against China. Since her recall to the team after a gap of 16 years, she has played three more times for New Zealand, bringing her total of international appearances to 14.

123. Rebecca Romero (1980-), *English rower and cyclist*

Rebecca Romero was born in Carshalton, Surrey in 1980.

Romero competed in the rowing events at the 2004 Olympics in Athens, where she won a silver medal in the quadruple sculls event. A year later, she was in the British team which won the gold medal in the quadruple sculls at the World Championships. However, a back injury put an end to her rowing and she retired from the sport in 2006, turning her attention instead to cycling.

Romero first competed at a UCI Track World Cup event in Moscow in December 2006, winning a silver medal. In 2007, she won her first medal at the World Cycling Championships, a silver in the 3KM pursuit event. A year later, at the 2008 UCI Track Cycling World Championships, she won the gold medal in both the individual pursuit event and the team pursuit event.

2008 also saw Romero competing at the Beijing Olympics, making her the first British woman to compete in two different sports at the Olympics; by winning the gold medal in the individual pursuit event, she became only the second woman, after the German Roswitha Krause (see Chapter 77), to win medals in two different sports at the Summer Olympics.

The dropping of the individual pursuit event from the Olympic programme meant Romero was unable to defend her title at the London Olympics in 2012. Instead, she now competes in Ironman events.

In 2009, Romero was awarded the MBE for her services to sport. In 2013, she set up Romero Performance, a sports performance consultancy organisation.

124. Melissa Ruscoe (1976-   ), *New Zealand footballer and rugby player*

Melissa Ruscoe was born in Taranaki, New Zealand in 1976.

Ruscoe's first international appearances were for the New Zealand football team back in 1994. Over the next 10 years, she played in 23 matches for New Zealand, captaining them on occasion and scoring twice for them; her matches included the qualifying matches for the 1999 Women's World Cup, but New Zealand lost out to Australia who secured the one place on offer for countries competing in the Oceania region.

In 2003, Ruscoe decided to switch to rugby, playing club rugby for Canterbury; a year later, she was making her debut for the national team as a loose forward. In 2006, she was a member of the New Zealand team which lifted the Women's Rugby World Cup; four years later New Zealand successfully defended their World Cup title, with Ruscoe as captain.

In 2011, Ruscoe was made a member of the New Zealand Order of Merit for her services to rugby.

With rugby and football played at much the same time of year, it is unusual to find anyone who has represented their country at both sports; in the case of Ruscoe, not only has she done this but she has also captained her country in both sports.

125. Deion Sanders (1967-   ), *American baseball player and American footballer*

Deion Sanders was born in Fort Myers, Florida in 1967.

Whilst at school, he excelled at American football, basketball and baseball, choosing to concentrate on American football and baseball in later life.

Sanders played baseball in the US's Major Baseball League from 1989 until 2001, playing for the New York Yankees in 1989 and 1990, the Atlanta Braves from 1991 to 1994, the Cincinnati Reds in 1994, 1995, 1997 and 2001 and the San Francisco Giants in 1995. Whilst with the Atlanta Braves, he played in four of the games against the Toronto Blue Jays in the World Series, which the Blue Jays won 4-2.

At American football, Sanders played as a defensive player, with the Atlanta Falcons from 1989 to 1993, with the San Francisco 49ers in 1994, with the Dallas Cowboys from 1995 to 1999, with the Washington Redskins in 2000, with the San Diego Chargers in 2002 and with the Baltimore Ravens in 2004 and 2005.

In 1989, whilst with the Atlanta Falcons, Sanders scored a touchdown in the NFL the same week as he scored a home run in the Major Baseball League for the New York Yankees. In 1994, he won the Super Bowl when the San Francisco 49ers beat the San Diego Chargers 49-26 and, a year later, won the Super Bowl again, this time with the Dallas Cowboys when they beat the Pittsburgh Steelers 27-17.

Sanders remains the only man to have competed in the Super Bowl and the World Series; efforts were often made to make him give up his baseball for American football and vice versa but he resisted them, citing that "football is my wife and baseball my mistress".

Sanders now works as an analyst with CBS Sports and the NFL Network.

126. Ricardo Saprissa (1901-1990), *Spanish footballer, hockey player and tennis player*

Ricardo Saprissa was born in San Salvador in El Salvador, the son of Catalan immigrants.

In the 1920s, Saprissa returned with his mother to live in Spain. In 1923 and 1924, he won the men's doubles in Spain's national tennis championships, following which he was selected to represent Spain at tennis in the mixed doubles and the men's doubles at the 1924 Olympics in Paris; in the men's doubles, Saprissa and his partner won their first match against Japan but lost in the last 16 round to South Africa and, in the mixed doubles, Saprissa and his partner lost in the last 32 round to Italy. Six years later, he made his only appearance for Spain in the Davis Cup when he played in the men's doubles match against Belgium, a match which Spain won 4-1, Saprissa winning his match in five sets.

From 1928 until 1932, Saprissa played football in defence for RCD Espanyol; in 1929, he played for them when they won the Copa del Rey, Spain's cup competition, beating Real Madrid 2-1 in the final.

Saprissa also played hockey for RCD Espanyol in the 1920s, at a time when they were one of Spain's leading hockey teams.

In 1932, Saprissa returned to Central America, to live in Costa Rica. In addition to coaching the Costa Rican national football team in 1935, 1938 and 1951, he also co-founded one of Costa Rica's most successful football clubs, Deportivo Saprissa, who play at the stadium named after him.

Saprissa died in 1990 at the age of 90.

127. Reggie Schwarz (1875-1918), *English rugby player and South African cricketer*

Reginald Schwarz was born in London in 1875.

After school, Schwarz went to Cambridge University where he won a blue at rugby, playing in the 1893 Varsity Match. Six years later, he was playing fly-half for England; his England debut was against Scotland, a game which the Scots won 5-0. Schwarz was next picked for England in 1901, when he played against Wales and Ireland; as with the game two years earlier against Scotland, both games were lost by England, with Wales winning 13-0 and Ireland winning 10-6.

The same year Schwarz played his last two games of rugby for England, he started playing cricket for Middlesex but, after two seasons with them, decided to emigrate to South Africa, where he played for Transvaal. In 1904, he was a member of the South African cricket team to tour England and whilst on tour, learned from its inventor, Bernard Bosanquet, how to bowl a googly. The googly became Schwarz's stock delivery and, when he returned to England with the South African team in 1907, he enjoyed considerable success on the tour, taking 137 wickets at an average of 11.70 and earning him the nomination of one of Wisden's five cricketers of the year.

In total, Schwarz played 20 Tests for South Africa between 1905 and 1912, scoring 374 runs with the bat, at an average of 13.85 and with a top score of 61 and taking 55 wickets at an average of 25.76, with best bowling figures of six for 47. In all first-class cricket, Schwarz played 125 matches, scoring 3,798 runs at an average of 22.60 with one century to his name, a score of 102 and having taken 398 wickets at an average of 17.58, with best bowling figures of eight for 55.

Schwarz retired from cricket in 1912 to pursue a career as a stockbroker. During the First World War, he served as a major in the King's Royal Rifle, fighting on the Western Front and, for his actions during the War, was awarded the Military Cross. Although he suffered two serious wounds, Schwarz survived the War, but died from the Spanish flu epidemic, whilst still in France, seven days after the Armistice was signed, at the age of 43.

128. Jack Sharp (1878-1938), *English footballer and cricketer*

John "Jack" Sharp was born in Hereford in 1878.

Sharp's football career began in 1897, with Aston Villa; after three seasons with them and after having made 23 appearances for them on the right wing and scoring 15 goals, he moved to Everton, playing 11 seasons for them. Whilst Sharp was at Everton, they were three times runners-up in the league championship but, in 1906, they had success in the F. A. Cup when they beat Newcastle 1-0 in the final; a year later, they were back in the final but, despite Sharp scoring for them, ended up losing 1-2 to Sheffield Wednesday.

Also whilst he was at Everton, Sharp was selected twice to play for England. His first match was in 1903 in England's Home Championships match against Ireland, which England won 4-0, with Sharp scoring one of the goals; his second game was two years later, against Scotland in the Home Championships, a game which England won 1-0. Sharp was one of the most thrilling wingers of his time; he played a total of 342 appearances for Everton and scored 80 goals for them.

Following his move from Aston Villa to Everton, Sharp started playing cricket for Lancashire. He continued to play for them until 1925; during the 1904 cricket season, he played in all their championship matches, when they won the championship without losing a game.

Five years later, he was selected for the England team against the touring Australians. In the first innings of his first Test, he top-scored with 61 as England were beaten and, in his third and final Test, which was drawn, he again top-scored with an innings of 105, his only Test century. In his three Tests, he scored 188 runs at an average of 47 and took three wickets at an average of 37.00.

By the time he retired from first-class cricket in 1925, he had played 441 matches, scoring 22,715 runs at an average of 31.11, with 38 centuries to his name and a top score of 237 and taking 441 wickets at an average of 27.41, with best bowling figures of nine for 77.

After retiring from playing professional sport, Sharp became a director of Everton, along with his brother Bertram who had played football with him at Aston Villa and Everton. Sharp also ran a sports shop in Liverpool supplying the football kit to both Everton and Liverpool.

Sharp died in 1938 at the age of 59.

129. Percy Sherwell (1880-1948), *South African cricketer and tennis player*

Percy Sherwell was born in Natal, South Africa in 1880.

Sherwell played his first game of first-class cricket in 1902 and continued playing until 1914, when the First World War put an end to his cricket. He was first picked to play for South Africa against the touring England team, in 1906 and was picked to captain the team on his debut; he captained South Africa in all 13 of the Test matches he played in – no other Test cricketer has played more Test matches than Sherwell and captained his team in every Test in which he has played.

Sherwell enjoyed immediate success in his first Test, which was also South Africa's first Test victory; Sherwell put on 48 with A D Nourse in a last wicket stand to win the match by one wicket.

Over his 13 Tests, Sherwell scored 427 runs at an average of 23.72 and scored one century, a score of 107 against England at Lord's in 1907; as wicketkeeper, he notched up 36 dismissals, 20 catches and 16 stumpings, which is the highest proportion of stumpings for a Test wicketkeeper with more than 20 dismissals to his name.

In total, Sherwell played 58 first-class games of cricket, scoring 1,808 runs at an average of 24.10, with three centuries and a highest score of 144; behind the stumps, he took 67 catches and accounted for 53 stumpings.

As well as being a Test cricketer, Sherwell was also a tennis champion, winning the South African men's singles title in 1904 and the men's doubles title in 1903 and 1904. He also represented South Africa against England in 1908/09.

Sherwell died in 1948 at the age of 67.

Author's notes. I have seen it reported that Sherwell also played football for South Africa but I have not seen any record to verify this.

Adbul Hafeez Kardar captained Pakistan in all 23 Test matches he played for them but only after having played three Tests for India not as captain and Kepler Wessels captained South Africa in all 16 Tests he played for them but only after having played 24 Tests for Australia not as captain.

130. Arnie Sidebottom (1954-), *English cricketer and footballer*

Arnold Sidebottom was born in Barnsley in 1954.

Sidebottom played cricket for Yorkshire from 1973 until 1991 and for Orange Free State from 1981 until 1984. After touring South Africa with a rebel tour in 1982, he was banned from Test cricket for three years but was selected to play for England against Australia for one Test in 1985. The Test was drawn and Sidebottom's contribution was two runs in his only innings and one wicket for 65 runs with his fast left-arm bowling; in his own words, his selection for England was after his sell-by date.

In all first-class cricket, Sidebottom played 228 games, scoring 4,508 runs at an average of 22.42, with one century, a score of 124 and took 596 wickets at an average of 24.42, with best figures of eight for 72.

Sidebottom was also a footballer, who turned professional with Manchester United in 1972. He made his first appearance for them as a defender in the 1973/74 season, at the end of which they were relegated from the First Division; the following season, which saw Manchester United gain promotion back to the First Division, he made a number of appearances for them following the injury to one of their international players but, in July 1975, after 20 appearances in total for the club, moved on a free transfer to Huddersfield Town. Over the next three seasons, he made a total of 61 appearances for Huddersfield Town before moving to Halifax Town. He retired from football in 1980 having played a total of 98 league fixtures for Manchester United, Huddersfield and Halifax. By virtue of his appearances for Manchester United in the 1973/74 season, Sidebottom can proudly claim to have played football in the top division of English football; however, in doing so, he qualified for a poll which was carried out by The Times in 2007, to identify the worst 50 footballers to have played in England's top football division; somewhat unflatteringly, Sidebottom was voted in at number 5; none of the four voted worse than him had the consolation though of having played cricket for England.

Sidebottom now coaches football and cricket at a school in Yorkshire. His son Ryan has also played cricket for England.

131. Jimmy Sinclair (1876-1913), *South African cricketer, rugby player and footballer*

James Hugh Sinclair was born in 1896 in Cape Province, South Africa.

Sinclair played 25 Tests for South Africa at cricket, from 1895 until 1910 and, by the end of his Test career, his hard hitting with the bat had brought him 1,069 runs at an average of 23.23 and a highest score of 106, whilst his fast bowling brought him 63 wickets at an average of 31.68, with best bowling figures of six for 26. The three centuries he scored in Test cricket were the first by any South African. On three occasions, he toured England with the South African team – in the case of the 1901 tour, he only made himself available after escaping from a POW camp after being captured by the Boers in the Second Boer War.

In all first-class cricket, Sinclair played 129 matches, scoring 4,483 runs at an average of 21.55, with six centuries and a top score of 136 and taking 491 wickets at an average of 21.43 and best figures of eight for 32. One record he holds for his batting is the furthest hit - a six he hit at the Wanderers Ground in Johannesburg ended up in a train on its way to Port Elizabeth, where the ball was eventually retrieved.

As well as playing cricket for South Africa, Sinclair also represented them in a game of football and played as a forward at rugby in the Test against Great Britain in 1903, which was drawn 10-10. He was also a skilful hockey player.

Sinclair died in 1913 at the age of 36.

132. Doug Smith (1924-1998), *Scottish rugby player, footballer and cricketer*

Doug Smith was born in Aberdeen in 1924.

Smith played on the wing at rugby and played for Scotland eight times between 1949 and 1953. He scored only one try, the second try in his second Test, a 6-3 win over Wales. He was selected for the British and Irish Lions tour to Australia in 1950 and played one Test for the Lions, which the Lions won 19-6; his tour came to an end when he broke his arm.

Smith was appointed manager of the Lions tour to Australia and New Zealand in 1971, with Carwyn James as coach. An early reversal, a defeat at the hands of Brisbane 24 hours after landing, caused New Zealand to write off the Lions' chances when they reached New Zealand but Smith remained confident, predicting that, of the four Tests, the Lions would win two, draw one and lose one. Smith's prediction proved to be spot on, inflicting upon the All Blacks the first ever series defeat at the hands of the Lions. Smith, who was a doctor by profession, explained to the media that the reason for the set-back in Brisbane was chronic circadian dysrhythmia; not many of those receiving this explanation recognised that this was the medical term for jet-lag. The success of the tour to New Zealand led the Lions' captain, Willie-John McBride, to credit Smith with being the finest of all Lions' managers.

As well as being a rugby international, Smith also played football for Aberdeen as an amateur and cricket for Aberdeenshire.

After his playing days were over, Smith continued practising as a doctor but also continued to be involved in rugby and, in 1986, he was appointed President of the Scottish Rugby Union.

Smith died in 1998 at the age of 73.

133. M. J. K. Smith (1933-   ), *English cricketer and rugby player*

Michael John Knight Smith, better known as M. J. K. Smith, was born in Westcotes, Leicestershire in 1933.

Smith first played cricket for Leicestershire in 1951 and played for them until he moved to Warwickshire as captain in 1957. In the meantime, he also played for Oxford University for whom he scored a century in each of his three Varsity matches.

By 1958, Smith had been selected to play for England and over the next nine years played in 50 Tests for them, captaining them in 25 of them, despite his dips in form with the bat never guaranteeing him a regular place. His running between the wickets has been described as unreliable but he still managed to accumulate 2,278 runs in Tests, at an average of 31.63, with three centuries and a top score of 121; he even picked up one wicket with his bowling which was only rarely used, his one wicket coming from 35.4 overs bowled and costing 128 runs. His close fielding though was more reliable than his running between the stumps and he finished taking 53 catches in his 50 Tests.

Smith's record as a Test cricketer does not tell of his reputation as a captain; Smith was a very popular captain, described as being very astute and perhaps best summed up by E. W. Swanton, who wrote of Smith that "he was thoughtful, unselfish, does not "fuss" them [the players] or panic, shows a grasp of the situation which they deem generally sensible, and at least gives an inspiring lead in the field".

In all first-class cricket, Smith played in 637 matches, scoring 39,832 runs at an average of 41.84, with 69 centuries and a top score of 204; his fielding brought him 593 catches.

Whilst at Oxford, Smith also played in two Varsity matches at rugby and, before graduating, had been picked to play for England; his only international was in 1956, as fly-half against Wales, a game which England lost 3-8.

When picked to play cricket for England two years later, he became the seventh and last Englishman to have played both cricket and rugby for England; in his Third Test, the other opening batsman was Arthur Milton (see Chapter 94), the twelfth and last Englishman to have played both cricket and football for England.

After retiring from playing cricket, Smith was an ICC match referee from 1991 until 1996 and Chairman of Warwickshire County Cricket from 1991 until 2003. In 1976, Smith was awarded the OBE for services to cricket. His son Neil has also captained Warwickshire at cricket and played in seven ODIs for England.

134. Betty Snowball (1908-1988), *English cricketer, lacrosse player and squash player*

Elizabeth Alexandra Snowball, known as Betty, was born in 1908 in Burnley.

Snowball opened the batting and kept wicket for England at cricket, playing in ten Tests between 1934 and 1949; her first Test match was the first played by women and she formed a formidable opening partnership with Myrtle Maclagan. In her ten Tests, Snowball scored 613 runs at an average of 40.86 and her only century, a score of 189 against New Zealand in 1935, was the highest by any woman until Sandya Agarwal's 190 for India in 1986 and remains the highest by an English women; in her ten Tests, she also took 13 catches and made eight stumpings.

Snowball also represented England at lacrosse and squash.

After retiring from playing cricket, Snowball umpired one Test match in 1951 and then taught maths and cricket at a prep school in Hertfordshire.

Snowball died in 1988 at the age of 80.

135. Reggie Spooner (1880-1961), *English cricketer and rugby player*

Reginald Spooner was born in Litherland, Lancashire in 1880.

Spooner first played cricket for Lancashire in 1899, before carrying out military service for three years, part of which involved him seeing action in the Second Boer War.

His success with the bat on his return saw Spooner selected to play for England in 1905 and, between 1905 and 1912, he played 12 Tests for England, in which he scored 481 runs at an average of 32.06 and one century, a score of 119.

Spooner continued playing for Lancashire up until 1923 but not on a regular basis due to a hunting accident in 1913 and business commitments. Despite this, he was invited to captain the MCC on their tour to Australia in 1920/21, an invitation he initially accepted but which he subsequently declined due to injury. Over a first-class career spanning 25 years, interrupted by his military service and the First World War, in which he served on the Western Front, Spooner scored a total of 13,681 runs at an average of 36.28, including 31 centuries and a top score of 247.

Spooner also played centre at rugby for Liverpool and, in 1903, was picked to play for England against Wales, a match Wales won 21-5. Spooner did not play rugby for England again.

Later in life, Spooner was appointed President of Lancashire County Cricket Club. He died in 1961 at the age of 80.

136. Jim Standen (1935-   ), *English cricketer and footballer*

Jim Standen was born in Edmonton, London in 1935.

Standen joined Arsenal as a goalkeeper in 1953 but did not make his league debut until 1957. With the Welsh goalkeeper Jack Kelsey also at Arsenal, Standen's appearances were limited and, in 1960 after 38 league appearances for Arsenal, he left them for Luton Town. At Luton, Standen experienced the same problem he had had at Arsenal, with Luton also having on their books the England goalie Ron Baynham. When West

Ham United's regular goalkeeper broke his leg in 1962, they took on Standen as cover, after only 36 league appearances for Luton.

Whilst at West Ham, Standen played 178 league games for them and his 57 cup fixtures include playing in the team which won the F. A. Cup in 1964 and the European Cup Winners Cup in 1965.

After a small spell with the Detroit Cougars, Standen joined Millwall for the 1969/70 season, playing eight games for them, before moving to Portsmouth, where he played 13 games over two seasons before retiring.

As a cricketer, Standen played in the Minor Counties Championship with Hertfordshire before joining Worcestershire in 1959. In the same year he won the F. A. Cup with West Ham, he won the County Championship with Worcestershire, heading their bowling averages with his right-arm medium pace bowling, taking 52 wickets at an average of 14.42. In his 12 seasons with Worcestershire, he took a total of 313 wickets at an average of 25.34, with best figures of seven for 30 and scored 2,092 runs at an average of 14.32 with a highest score of 92 not out.

After retiring from football in 1972, Standen ran a sports shop in Surrey before emigrating to California.

137. Jackie Stewart (1939-   ), *Scottish shot and motor racer*

Sir John Young "Jackie" Stewart was born in West Dunmartonshire in 1939.

Stewart took up clay pigeon shooting when he was 14, winning his first competition in his first year at the sport. Before long, he became a member of the Scottish shooting team, winning the British, Welsh and Scottish skeet shooting championships and the Coupe des Nations European championships.

In 1960, Stewart was expected to win a place in the British trap shooting team competing in the Olympics that year but, on his 21st birthday when the final qualifying competition was held, he shot his worst round of the year and missed qualification by one target.

Following this disappointment, Stewart turned his hand to motor racing. By 1964, he was racing in Formula 3 for the Tyrrell racing team and a year later competed in his first Formula 1 race, racing with the BRM team in the South African Grand Prix. 1965 also saw him record his first Formula 1 victory, the Italian Grand Prix.

In 1968, Stewart switched to the Tyrrell Matra team and in 1969, with six wins in his 11 races, won his first World Championship title. In 1971, he again won six races out of his 11 starts, to win the World Championship for the second time. The Brazilian Emerson Fittipaldi took the title in 1972 but Stewart bounced back in 1973 to claim his third World Championship title, with five wins in his 14 races – his final and 15th race of the year was due to be the US Grand Prix but Stewart retired from the race before the start following the death of his teammate Francois Cevert in practice.

Stewart stopped racing at the end of the 1973 season; over all, he started in 99 Formula 1 races, winning 27 of them; his three World Championship titles are the most by any Briton, being one more than the two titles won by Graham Hill, Jim Clark and Lewis Hamilton, although Hamilton is on course to match Stewart's record.

After crashing in Spa in 1966, Stewart became a leading advocate for safety in motor racing, something he continued after his retirement from racing - he has been credited with doing more than anyone else to make Formula 1 racing safer. After retiring from racing, he also spent time commentating on racing before, in 1997, returning to Formula 1 with his own team, in partnership with his son. Stewart is also credited with being responsible for introducing the idea of showering the podium with champagne after victories, although not intentionally; after one of his wins in France, the double magnum which was presented to him had been left out in the sun and, on uncorking it, the champagne went everywhere.

In 1973, his final year of racing, Stewart was the BBC's Sports Personality of the Year and, in 2001, was knighted for his services to motor racing.

Stewart's older brother Jimmy also raced motor cars and took part in the 1953 British Grand Prix.

138. Micky Stewart (1932-), *English cricketer and footballer*

Micky Stewart was born in Herne Hill in 1932.

Stewart made his debut for Surrey at cricket in 1954 and, in his second game for them, scored his first century, against the touring Pakistanis. His first five years at Surrey saw them win the County Championship each year but his sixth County Championship came much later, in 1971 when he was captain. By 1962, he was picked for England and over the next two years played for them eight times. In his eight Test matches, he scored 385 runs at an average of 35, with a top score of 87. By the time he retired in 1972, after 10 years as Surrey captain, he had played 530 first-class matches, scoring 26,491 runs at an average of 32.90, with 49 centuries and a top score of 227 not out.

Stewart also was a fine close fielder; his seven catches in one innings in a match against Northamptonshire in 1957 is the equal highest by anyone other than a wicketkeeper and his 77 catches in the 1957 season second only to Wally Hammond's 78 in the 1928 season.

Stewart was also a footballer. He played as an amateur for Corinthian Casuals and played for England in an amateur international against France in 1956. He had hoped to represent Great Britain at the 1956 Olympics but was ruled to be ineligible on the grounds that he was a professional cricketer; as a consequence, he turned professional and joined Charlton Athletic, who already had three Kent cricketers on their books.

After his playing days were over, Stewart served as the Surrey manager from 1979 until 1986, when he was appointed England's first full-time manager, a position he held until 1992; in 1992, he was appointed Director of Coaching for the English Cricket Board, a position he held for six years. In 1998, Stewart was awarded the OBE for services to cricket.

Stewart's son, Alec, also played cricket for England, in 133 Tests, the most by any Englishman and in 170 one day internationals.

139. Andrew Stoddard (1863-1915), *English cricketer and rugby player*

Andrew Stoddard was born in South Shields in 1863.

Stoddard first played cricket for Middlesex in 1885; a year after his debut, Stoddard was considering turning his back on cricket by joining his brother in Colorado but he changed his mind after a purple patch which saw him score 485 runs in a day for Hampstead, then the highest ever score in cricket, followed by an innings of 207 three days later in Hampstead's next match. Two years later, he was picked to play for England. Over the next 10 years he played in 16 Tests, captaining England in eight of them. He scored 996 runs at an average of 35.57, with two centuries and a top score of 173; his two wickets bowling cost 47 apiece.

Stoddard retired from playing cricket in 1900 by which time he had played 309 first-class matches. His 16,738 runs were scored at an average of 32.12 and included 26 centuries and a top score of 221; he enjoyed more success bowling in first-class matches than in Tests, taking 278 wickets in total, at an average of 23.63 and with best figures of seven for 67.

Stoddard also played rugby for England as a three-quarter. He played in ten Tests between 1885 and 1893, captaining them on four occasions and scoring two tries and making one conversion. As well as playing for Blackheath, he was also a founding member of the Barbarians Rugby Club and captained them in their first ever game; he also helped organise the first British Lions tour to Australia in 1888, which included a game of Australian rules football which Stoddard played in. Whilst on tour, Stoddard assumed the captaincy when Robert Seddon died in a sculling accident.

Away from sport, Stoddard worked in the Stock Exchange and as secretary of the Queens Club. Stoddard died in 1915 at the age of 52, when he took his own life at a time when his health was failing him and his debts were mounting. He remains though the only Englishman to have represented England on at least ten occasions at both cricket and rugby.

140. Frank Stoker (1867-1939), *Irish rugby player and tennis player*

Frank Stoker was born in Dublin in 1867.

Stoker won the Irish men's doubles championships at tennis in 1890, 1891, 1893, 1894 and 1895; with his partner Joshua Pim, he also won the Wimbledon men's doubles title in 1890 and 1893. Stoker also entered the men's singles at Wimbledon in 1891 and 1893; in 1891, he gave a walk-over to Wilfred Baddeley who went on to win the title and, in 1893, lost in the second round.

His performances in 1892 earned him a ranking of number 7 in the world.

Stoker also played rugby as a forward and played five games for Ireland between 1886 and 1891; his five matches consisted of two against Scotland, two against Wales and one against the New Zealand Natives, but he was only on the winning side in one of these matches, the fixture against Wales in 1888.

In his professional life Stoker was a dentist. He died at the age of 71 in 1939 but remains one of only two rugby internationals to have won a Wimbledon title, the other being James Cecil Parke (see Chapter 107).

141. Sarah Storey (1977-   ), *English Paralympian swimmer and cyclist*

Dame Sarah Storey (nee Bailey) was born in 1977; at birth, she was left without a functioning left hand.

Storey's Paralympics career started in 1992 at the age of 14, when she took part in swimming events, winning two golds, three silvers and a bronze. At the 1996 Paralympic Games, she won three more golds, another silver and another bronze in the swimming events. Storey also competed in swimming events at the next two Paralympic Games and, although she was unable to add to her tally of gold medals, she did add two more silvers at the 2000 Games and two more silvers and a bronze at the 2004 Games.

Storey also enjoyed considerable success in swimming events at International Paralympic Committee World Championships between 1994 and 2002, winning a total of five gold medals, five silver medals and five bronze medals.

After the 2004 Paralympic Games, Storey started competing in cycling events. At the 2008 Games, she won one gold in road cycling and one in track cycling and four years later in London, won two golds in road cycling events and two golds in track cycling events. Her appearances at five International Paralympic Committee World Championships between 2005 and 2014 have brought her a total of 15 gold medals in road and track cycling events, as well as two silvers and two bronzes.

Storey has also been able to compete successfully against athletes without disabilities. As well as winning three national track cycling titles, when competing in the 2010 Commonwealth Games, she became the first disabled cyclist to compete for England at such Games.

Storey was awarded the MBE in 1998 and the OBE in 2009; after the 2012 Games in London, Storey was awarded a DBE, making her a Dame Commander of the Order of the British Empire. In 2012, Storey took part on Celebrity Mastermind, choosing as her specialist subject Sex & The City.

142. John Willie Sutcliffe (1868-1947), *English footballer and rugby player*

John William Sutcliffe was born in Shibden in 1868.

Sutcliffe played full-back and centre for Bradford Rugby Club before moving to Heckmondwike; whilst at Heckmondwike, Sutcliffe was picked to play for England in 1889 against the touring New Zealand Natives. This match was Sutcliffe's only rugby international; because of the scoring system at the time, England won the match 7-0 having scored five tries (each of which was worth one point) and having converted one of the tries (which was worth two points) to New Zealand's none, with Sutcliffe scoring one of the tries and kicking the conversion.

Following the suspension of Heckmondwike by the RFU on suspicion of professionalism, Sutcliffe decided to play football instead. He joined Bolton Wanderers and played in goal for them for 14 years, making 332 league appearances and playing for them in the F. A. Cup Final in 1894 when they lost 4-1 to Notts County.

After short spells with Millwall and Manchester United, Sutcliffe joined Plymouth Argyle, for whom he played 214 league fixtures before ending his playing days with Southend United.

Sutcliffe made his football debut for England in 1893 and, over a ten year period, played a total of five matches for England.

After retiring as a player, Sutcliffe managed the Dutch team Vitesse before taking on a coaching role at Bradford City.

Sutcliffe died in 1947 at the age of 79 and he remains the last of only three Englishmen who have played football and rugby for England.

143. Clare Taylor (1965-   ), *English cricketer and footballer*

Clare Taylor was born in Huddersfield in 1965.

Taylor was an opening bowler who bowled medium pace. She played for Yorkshire in the English summers and Otago in the English winters. She played her first one day international for England in 1988 and, over 18 years, played in 105 ODIs for England, including in five World Cups. Her first Test came in 1995 and, over her nine year Test career, played in 16 Tests. She was a member of the England team which won the Women's Cricket World Cup in 1993 and, in taking 25 wickets in her 16 Test matches and 102 wickets in her 105 ODIs, became the first English woman to take 100 wickets in international matches.

Taylor started her football career with Bronte Ladies before joining Knowsley United, which then became Liverpool Ladies; she played for Knowsley and Liverpool in the 1994, 1995 and 1996 F. A. Women's Cup Finals, on each occasion on the losing side. Taylor played her first game for England, as a sweeper, against Germany in 1990. She also played for England in the 1995 World Cup, thereby becoming the only woman to have played in cricket and football World Cups for England. When winning the cricket World Cup in 1993 at Lord's, she also played that year at Wembley in the F. A. Women's Premier League Cup Final.

Taylor was awarded the MBE in 2000 for services to women's sport.

Author's note – Clare Taylor is not the Claire Taylor who also represented England at cricket between 1998 and 2011.

144. Johnny Taylor (1895-1971), *Australian cricketer and rugby player*

John Morris Taylor was born in Stanmore, New South Wales in 1895.

In the words of Wisden, Taylor was a polished batsman and a brilliant fieldsman at cover. He played in 20 Tests for Australia between 1920 and 1926, scoring 997 runs at an average of 35.60; his 19 overs in Tests brought him one wicket for 45 runs. When, in 1924, he scored his one and only Test century, an innings of 108, he put on 127 runs in a tenth wicket partnership with Arthur Mailey, which remained the highest tenth wicket partnership for Australia against England until beaten by Philip Hughes and Ashton Agar in 2013.

As well as representing Australia, Taylor also played for New South Wales from 1913 until 1927; over a career consisting of 135 first-class matches, he scored 6,274 runs at an average of 33.37, with 11 centuries and a highest score of 180; the only wicket he took with his bowling was the one he took in a Test match.

Taylor also played fly-half at rugby and was picked to play in two matches for Australia in 1922 against the touring New Zealand Maoris. Despite Australia scoring six tries to the Maoris' four, Australia lost the first match 22-25, with Taylor scoring a try and kicking two conversions; had five points been awarded for a try as is the case nowadays rather than three as was the case back in 1926, the result would have been different. Australia however avenged the defeat two days later when they won 28-13 with Taylor scoring another try and kicking a conversion and a penalty.

During the First World War, Taylor served with the First Australian Imperial force as an artillery gunner. Taylor died in hospital in 1971 after a heart attack, at the age of 75.

145. Jacob Tullin Thams (1898-1954), *Norwegian sailor and skier*

Jacob Tullin Thams was born in Norway in 1898.

Thams took part in the first Winter Olympics, in 1924 in Grenoble, winning the gold medal in the ski jumping event. Two years later, he won the World Championship gold medal in ski jumping, which also earned him the Holmenkoller Medal, the highest award given to a Norwegian skier. Along with fellow Norwegian Sigmund Ruud, Thams developed the Kongsberger technique for ski jumpers, whereby the upper body was bent at the hip, the arms stretched out in front and the skis parallel, a technique which saw ski jumpers more than double the distance they previously jumped and which lasted until the 1950s when superseded by new techniques.

In 1936, Thams was a member of the Norwegian team which won the silver medal at the Berlin Olympics in the eight metre sailing event. In winning medals at both a Winter Olympic Games and a Summer Olympic Games, Thams became only the third person to do so and, after Eddie Eagen (see Chapter 43) only the second to do so in different events.

Thams died in 1954 at the age of 66.

Author's note:

Sweden's Gillis Grafstrom won the gold medal in the figure skating event at the Summer Olympics in 1920 when figure skating was an event at the Summer Olympics; from 1924, figure skating became an event at the Winter Olympics and Grafstrom won the gold medal at the 1924 and 1928 Winter Olympics – he therefore won gold medals at both the Summer Olympics and the Winter Olympics but his medals were only for one event.

146. Keith Thomson (1941-　), *New Zealand cricketer and hockey player*

Keith Thomson was born in Methven, New Zealand in 1941.

Thomson played hockey for Canterbury at centre-half and at inside-right from 1959 until 1974; he was first picked for the New Zealand national team, the Black Sticks, in 1961 and over the next 10 years played in 28 games for them, including in the 1968 Olympics when he played in eight of their nine games, scoring in three of them; despite being one of only two teams to be unbeaten team in their group games, the other being Pakistan who won all their matches and the gold medal, New Zealand ended in seventh place overall.

Thomson also played cricket for Canterbury, from the 1959/60 season through to the 1973/74 season. In 1968, he was picked to play in the second and third Tests of a four Test series against the touring Indians; he scored 69 in his first innings of his first Test but, after a duck in the second innings of his second Test, was not picked again to play for the national

154

team. In his two Tests, he scored 94 runs at an average of 31.33, with his 69 on debut being his highest score; although he was not picked for his bowling, Thomson was given the chance to bowl in his second Test as India needed only 59 runs in their second innings to win the Test and picked up the wicket of Farouk Engineer; in his 3.3 overs, he conceded just nine runs. By the time he retired, Thomson had played in 71 first-class games of cricket, scoring 3,134 runs at an average of 28.33, with five centuries to his name and a top score of 136 not out. He only added four more wickets to his one Test wicket, his wickets coming at a cost of 49.20 apiece.

After he stopped playing professional sport, Thomson became a hockey umpire and umpired in two international matches.

147. Dick Thornett (1940-2011), *Australian water polo player and rugby player*

Dick Thornett was born in Sydney in 1940.

The first sport in which Thornett represented Australia was water polo, when he was a member of their team taking part in the 1960 Olympics.

A year after the Olympics, Thornett was playing lock at rugby union for Randwick DRUFC, a club he played for for two years before switching codes and turning professional. Whilst with Randwick, he was selected to play for Australia and was capped 11 times. Thornett's international career at rugby union got off to a flying start with him winning his first two matches and scoring on his debut; thereafter it went downhill with two of his remaining Tests being drawn and the other seven lost.

In 1963, Thornett joined the rugby league side Parramatta, for whom he played 168 games in his nine seasons with them, scoring 35 tries. He also represented New South Wales on 12 occasions between 1963 and 1969 and played in 11 Tests between 1963 and 1968, including as vice-captain in Australia's 1968 World Cup winning team. In 1972, he joined Eastern Suburbs but only played a handful of games for them before retiring after one season.

Thornett's older brothers, Ken and John, were also rugby players. John played rugby union for Australia and played in nine of the Tests in which Dick played, whilst Ken played rugby league and played in three Tests alongside Dick.

Thornett died in 2011 at the age of 71.

148. Jim Thorpe (1888-1953), *American athlete, baseball player and American footballer*

Jim Thorpe was born in Oklahoma in 1888.

Up until 1910, Thorpe played minor league baseball but the club he played for was disbanded, making him a free agent. In 1913, he joined the New York Giants, for whom he played only intermittently up until 1918, having also played during this time for the Milwaukee Brewers and the Cincinnati Reds. His final major league baseball team was the Boston Braves for whom he played in 1919; he spent his last four years of baseball playing in minor league but not before having played 289 games in the major league.

In 1912, Thorpe competed in the 1912 Olympics in Stockholm, taking part in the pentathlon and decathlon events. In the pentathlon, he came first in the long jump, the 200 metres, the discus and the 1,500 metres events and third in the fifth event, the javelin, to win the gold medal. In the decathlon, he also won four of the events as well as finishing in the top four in all ten events, to secure the gold medal in that event as well.

The year after Thorpe won his Olympic gold medals, it was reported that Thorpe had been a professional baseball player and, as a consequence, Thorpe was stripped of his Olympic titles on the grounds of his status as a professional sportsman, even though this was not raised within 30 days after the Games' closing ceremony as was required under the IOC's own rules. Almost 30 years after his death, the Jim Thorpe Foundation mounted a campaign to have Thorpe re-instated as Olympic champion and their appeal to the IOC resulted in the IOC declaring Thorpe champion in both the pentathlon and decathlon events, albeit as co-champion in each case with the athlete who had originally been runner-up to him.

After having been awarded All-American honours in 1911 and 1912 in American football whilst at college, Thorpe first played as a professional footballer in 1913 for the Pine Village Pros. In 1915, he joined the Canton Bulldogs, for whom he continued to play up until 1920, the year the American Professional Football Association (the APFA) was formed; the Canton Bulldogs were one of the APFA's original teams – two years later, the APFA became the National Football League (the NFL).

Between 1921 and 1923, Thorpe played American football for the all native-American team, the Oorang Indians, Thorpe's grandmothers both being native Indians. Thorpe continued to play American football until 1929, retiring at the age of 41. As well as playing American football for a native American team, Thorpe also formed and played in the mid-1920s for an all native-American basketball team. Other sports at which Thorpe excelled include boxing, golf, lacrosse, rowing and swimming.

After his career as a professional sportsman came to an end, Thorpe tried his luck at Hollywood, where he featured in more than 60 films.

Thorpe died in 1953 from heart failure at the age of 64. In a poll of sports fans carried out by ABC Sports in 2000, Thorpe was voted the greatest athlete of the 20th century from a list of 15 athletes, which included other great sportsmen such as Jesse Owen, Babe Ruth, Jack Nicklaus and Muhammed Ali; however, the list though only included one sportsman or sportswoman who was not an American citizen, namely the Brazilian footballer Pele and, as the voters targeted were American, perhaps the only correct conclusion one can draw from this poll is that, in the eyes of American sports fans, Thorpe was the greatest American athlete of the 20th century.

149. Eric Tindill (1910-2010), *New Zealand cricketer and rugby player*

Eric Tindill was born in Nelson, New Zealand in 1910.

Tindall was a wicketkeeper/batsman who first played first-class cricket for Wellington in the 1932/33 season, scoring a century on his debut. In 1937, he was picked for the tour to England and played in all three of the Tests; on the return journey to New Zealand after the tour, Tindill played in the game against South Australia, catching Don Bradman facing his first ball on the second morning of the match, for 11 – it was the only time Bradman ever played against, and the only time he was ever dismissed by, a New Zealand team.

After serving in North Africa in the War, Tindill continued to play cricket for Wellington until 1950. He also played in two more Tests, the first one against Australia in 1946 and the second against England in 1947; the Test against Australia was a low scoring affair, with New Zealand dismissed for 42 in their first innings and 54 in their second innings, with Tindill's score of 13 being the second highest score in the second innings.

Tindill's Test record did not flatter him; in his five Tests, he scored only 73 runs at an average of 9.12 with a top score of 37 not out; his wicketkeeping brought him six catches and one stumping. He played a total of 69 games of first-class cricket, in which he scored 3,127 runs at an average of 30.35, with six centuries and a highest score of 149 and took 96 catches and made 33 stumpings.

Tindill also played rugby for Wellington as fly-half and centre and, as with his debut at cricket, had a memorable first game; his debut was against the All Blacks before they set off on their 1932 tour to Australia – Wellington won 36-23 with Tindill scoring a try against his national team.

Tindill was picked for the All Blacks' tour to England in 1936 but only played in one Test, New Zealand's first defeat at the hands of the English, a match in which Charlie Oliver (see Chapter 104) and Tuppy Owen-Smith (see Chapter 103) also played and in which famously Prince Alexander

Obolensky scored two tries in a 13-0 victory. Tindill was unavailable for the All Blacks' tour to South Africa in 1937 as he was touring England with the cricket team. He was however available for the 1938 tour to Australia but only selected for three of the matches against Australian States. Altogether, Tindill played 17 matches for New Zealand, scoring 24 points with his six drop goals – drop goals were then worth four points each – but his only Test was the one against England in 1936.

As well as playing cricket and rugby for Wellington, he also played football for them in 1927 and was a founding member of the Wellington Table Tennis Association in 1932.

Having qualified as an accountant, Tindill worked in the Civil Service but still found time to referee rugby matches and umpire cricket matches. Uniquely, he is not only the only person to have played Test rugby and Test cricket for New Zealand but also the only one to have also refereed a Test rugby fixture and umpired a Test cricket match.

In 1981, Tindill was awarded the OBE for services to rugby and cricket; he died in 2010 at the age of 99; immediately prior to his death, he was the oldest ever Test cricketer, a record that he held until March 2011 when the South African Norman Gordon became the oldest, and the oldest surviving, Test cricketer.

150. Brent Todd (1964-), *New Zealand rugby league player and water polo player*

Brent Todd was born in 1964.

Todd first represented New Zealand at water polo before embarking upon his rugby league career.

Todd was a prop forward at rugby league and first played for Canterbury in 1985 but, after two years, crossed the Tasman Sea to join the Canberra Raiders. Over the next five years, Todd played in 91 matches for them, including in the Winfield Cup Grand Finals in 1987, 1989, 1990 and

1991 – the Raiders won the Cup in 1989 and 1990 but were runners-up in 1987 and 1991. During his time with the Raiders, Todd also had a short spell with Wakefield Trinity, playing nine matches for them in the 1988/89 season. In 1992, he joined the Gold Coast Seagulls, playing 34 games for them.

Todd received his first international call-up in 1985 and played his last rugby league game for New Zealand in 1993, having played in 28 Tests and scoring two tries for them.

Since retiring as a player, Todd has been a rugby league commentator on television but, after being involved in a poker machine fraud scheme, was declared bankrupt and sentenced to 12 months detention at home in 2007.

151. Thami Tsolekile (1980-), *South African hockey player and cricketer*

Thami Tsolekile was born in Cape Town in 1980.

In 1999, Tsolekile scored on his debut when becoming the first black South African to represent his country at hockey.

By 1999, Tsolekile was playing first-class cricket and, perhaps benefitting from the South African policy of positive discrimination, was selected to play in three Tests as wicketkeeper at the expense of Mark Boucher. In the three Tests in which Tsolekile played, two were against India and one against England but his performances in scoring 47 runs at an average of 9.40 with a top score of 22 and in taking six catches were not enough to prevent Boucher being re-selected ahead of him.

Tsolekile is still playing first-class cricket and, by the end of 2014/15, had played in 160 first-class matches in which he has scored 5,844 runs at an average of just over 30, with six centuries and a highest score of 159 and taken 499 catches and made 36 stumpings; one of his centuries came in 2009 in his third match for Lions when he and opener Stephen Cook put on 365 runs for the sixth wicket, a South African record – Cook went on to score 390, the highest innings by a South African and the highest innings in South Africa.

152. Maurice Turnbull (1906-1944), *Welsh rugby player, squash player and hockey player and English cricketer*

Maurice Turnbull was born in Cardiff in 1906.

Turnbull first played cricket for Glamorgan in 1924, whilst he was still at school. After leaving school, he went to Cambridge University and captained their cricket team in 1929; a year later he was captain of Glamorgan, a position he retained until the Second World War broke out in 1939.

1929 saw Turnbull picked for the MCC tour for Australia and New Zealand. Turnbull made his Test debut for England in 1930 against New Zealand and, over the next seven years, played in eight more Tests for England; in his nine Tests, Turnbull scored 224 runs at an average of 20.36 with a top score of 61. During a first-class career ranging from 1924 until 1939, Turnbull played 388 games, scoring 17,544 runs at an average of 29.78, with 29 centuries and a top score of 233; his four first-class wickets were rather expensive at 88.75 apiece.

Whilst at Cambridge, Turnbull also won a blue in hockey and, in 1929, played hockey for Wales. Although Turnbull was also a member of Cambridge University Rugby Club, he did not win a blue at rugby, but this did not prevent him playing scrum-half for Cardiff and London Welsh and, in 1933, he was selected to play for Wales in the Home Nations Championships; his first Test saw Wales record a narrow victory over England, Wales's first win over England at Twickenham but he was injured for the next match against Scotland; fit again for the Ireland fixture, Turnbull won back his place but, after a defeat at the hands of the Irish, 11 of the Welsh team were dispensed with, including Turnbull.

In addition to cricket, hockey and rugby, Turnbull played squash at which he was good enough to win the South Wales title.

During the War, Turnbull served in the Welsh Guards reaching the rank of major; he died after the Normandy Landings in 1944 at the age of 38. Accounts differ as to how he died, one account being that he was shot by a sniper and another being that he was shot during a German counter-attack as he was trying to immobilise a lead vehicle as tanks and soldiers were heading towards his unit in Montchamp. Turnbull's father, Philip, also played hockey for Wales and his brother, Bernard, rugby for Wales. Turnbull remains the only person to have played cricket for England and rugby for Wales.

153. Percy Twentyman-Jones (1876-1954), *South African cricketer and rugby player*

Percy Twentyman-Jones was born in Beaufort, South Africa in 1876.

Twentyman-Jones played on the wing at rugby for Western Province and, in 1896, was picked to play for South Africa in the Test series against the touring British Isles team. Twentyman-Jones played in the first Test, which the British Isles won 8-0, missed the second Test, but played in the third and fourth Tests. Twentyman-Jones scored his one and only international try in the third Test which South Africa lost 3-9; the fourth Test, which South Africa won 5-0, was South Africa's first Test victory.

Twentyman-Jones also played cricket for Western Province and, after scoring 33 and 50 – the 50 being out of a second innings total of 80 - against the touring Australian team in 1902, was selected to play for South Africa against Australia in the third Test; Twentyman-Jones was not able to repeat the form he had shown when playing for Western Province and, after scoring ducks in both innings of the Test, was not picked again. In total, Twentyman-Jones played only 10 games of first-class cricket, in which he scored 306 runs at an average of 18 and with a top score of 53.

Twentyman-Jones qualified as a lawyer in 1898 and subsequently became a judge. He died in 1954 at the age of 77.

154. Clive van Ryneveld (1928-   ), *South African cricketer and English rugby player*

Clive van Ryneveld was born in Cape Town in 1928.

Van Ryneveld attended Oxford University on a Rhodes Scholarship and represented them in the 1947, 1948 and 1949 Varsity rugby matches against Cambridge. Whilst at Oxford, he was selected to play centre for England in the 1949 Five Nations and played in all four games; England finished second after losing to Ireland and Wales, with van Ryneveld scoring a try against Ireland and two against Scotland.

Van Ryneveld also played cricket whilst at Oxford, having already played for Western Province since 1946. As with rugby, he played in three Varsity matches, in 1948, 1949 and 1950, before returning to South Africa. In 1951, van Ryneveld was picked for the South Africa tour to England and over the next seven years, played 19 Tests for South Africa, as an all-rounder who could not only bat and bowl leg spin but who was also an outstanding fielder. His 19 Tests brought him 724 runs with the bat at an average of 26.81 with a highest score of 83 and his 17 wickets came at 39.47 apiece with best figures of four for 67. By the time he retired from playing for Western Province at the end of the 1962/63 season, he had played in 101 games of first-class cricket, scoring 4,803 runs at an average of 30.20, with four centuries and a highest score of 150 and taken 206 wickets at an average of 30.24, with best figures of eight for 48.

Before retiring from cricket, van Ryneveld went into politics and was elected to Parliament in 1957 as a member of the United Party; two years later, along with 11 other MPs, he founded the Progressive Party which adopted a more aggressive stance against apartheid but all but one of the members of the Progressive Party, including van Ryneveld, lost their seats at the next election in 1961, Helen Suzman being the only one to retain her seat.

After leaving the world of politics, van Ryneveld worked for a merchant bank until his retirement in 1988.

155. Rudi van Vuuren (1972-), *Namibian cricketer and rugby player*

Rudi van Vuuren was born in Windhoek, Namibia in 1972.

Van Vuuren played cricket for Namibia in the 2003 cricket World Cup, playing in five of their six group matches, all of which they lost. In his five games, van Vuuren scored 26 runs, with 14 coming in his first game against Pakistan and 12 not out in his second game against England – thereafter it was 0 not out against India followed by two ducks against Australia and Holland; the game against Australia, who went on to win the World Cup, was the heaviest defeat in terms of runs at any World Cup, Australia winning by 245 runs and with van Vuuren conceding 28 runs in one of his overs; at the time, this was the most runs conceded in one over at the World Cup, a record which was broken four years later when Herschelle Gibbs hit six sixes in an over. Van Vuuren managed to take eight wickets, including five against England and two against India – the two against India were the only wickets to fall as they scored 311 for 2 in their 50 overs, but the two wickets taken by van Vuuren were the prized wickets of Virender Sehwag and Sachin Tendulkar.

In the same year van Vuuren was selected to play in the cricket World Cup, he was also picked as a member of the Namibian squad playing in the rugby World Cup. Van Vuuren did not play in Namibia's first three games but came on as a substitute, at full-back, in their last game against Romania, a game which Romania won 37-7. Van Vuuren's appearance against Romania made him the first man to compete in the final stages of the cricket World Cup and the rugby World Cup in the same year.

Away from sport, van Vuuren is a physician and a committed conservationist; in 2006, he and his wife, along with two friends, started the Naankuse Foundation to protect and improve the lives of the people and wildlife of Namibia.

156. George Vernon (1856-1902), *English cricketer and rugby player*

George Vernon was born in London in 1856.

Vernon played most of his cricket for Middlesex, playing 103 games for them between 1878 and 1895. He was selected to tour Australia on the first ever Ashes tour, in 1882/83 and played in only one of the Tests on that tour. In a match Australia won by nine wickets, Vernon batted at number 11, scoring 11 not out and 3 but, despite being put in to bat at the bottom of the batting order, was not called upon to try out his slow, underarm bowling.

As well as playing just the one Test for England, and for Middlesex, Vernon also played for the MCC, the Gentlemen of England and the South of England and, by the time he retired, had played a total of 240 first-class matches, scoring 7,070 runs at an average of 19.10, with four centuries and a top score of 160.

Vernon also played rugby as a forward for Blackheath and was picked for England in five internationals between 1878 and 1881; Vernon's first match, against Scotland, was drawn but the other four matches, three against Ireland and another one against Scotland, were all won by England.

Away from sport, Vernon was a barrister; he died in Ghana from malaria in 1902, at the age of 46.

157. Arumugam Vijiaratnam (1921-), *Singaporean footballer, cricketer, rugby player and hockey player*

Arumugam Vijiaratnam was born in Singapore in 1921.

The Second World War and the Japanese occupation of Singapore put Vijiaratnam's sporting career on hold but, once the War was over, Vijiaratnam played football, cricket and rugby for Singapore in fixtures against neighbouring Malaya.

After an injury in football, Vijiaratnam took up hockey and was selected for the Singapore team at the 1956 Olympics. Although the Singapore team suffered a heavy defeat at the hands of the eventual winners India in their group match, they had the satisfaction of coming second in their group after wins of 5-0 over Afghanistan and 6-1 over the USA. Second place in their group though was not enough to see them through to the knock-out stages and, instead, they played in another group of four, to determine fifth to eighth places; after losing all their games in this group, Singapore were ranked eighth, Vijiaratnam having played in four of their six matches overall.

Vijiaratnam mixed his sporting achievements with work and his work earned him the distinction of becoming Singapore's first engineer; later in life, he took on a management role at the Port of Singapore Authority before becoming the first Pro-Chancellor at Nanyang Technical University.

158. Ellsworth Vines (1911-1994), *American tennis player and golfer*

Henry Ellsworth Vines was born in Los Angeles in 1911.

As an amateur tennis player, Vines won three Grand Slam singles titles. His first title was the US championships in 1931, a title he successfully defended in 1932, the same year he won Wimbledon, beating Britain's Henry Austin in the final; a year later, Vines reached the Wimbledon final again but lost to the Australian Jack Crawford. Vines also won three Grand Slam doubles titles, the men's doubles at the US championships in 1932 and at the Australian championships in 1933 and the mixed doubles at the US championships in 1933.

By 1934, Vines had turned professional and, as a professional, won five of the major professional tournaments, the Wembley Pro tournament in 1934, 1935 and 1936, the French Pro tournament in 1935 and the US Pro tournament in 1939, when he beat Britain's Fred Perry (see Chapter 112) in the final.

From 1934 to 1938, Vines was the World Pro champion, a title he lost in 1939 to Don Budge, who had turned pro after becoming the first man to win the Grand Slam of tennis majors.

Following his loss of number 1 ranking to Budge, Vines stopped playing tennis professionally and concentrated on golf. He competed in the British Amateur championships in 1939 and the US Amateur championships in 1941, before turning professional in 1942. As a professional golfer, Vines won three tournaments and, on 14 occasions, took part in the majors. Of the 14 majors he played in, three were the Masters, his best result at the Masters being tied 24th place in 1947, four were the US Open, where his best result was tied 14th place in 1948 and 1949 and seven were at the US PGA, where his best result was in 1951 when he reached the semi-final – up until 1957, the US PGA championships were a knock-out matchplay competition; in the semi-final, Vines lost to Walter Burkemo at the first extra hole, having been level after 36 holes, Burkemo going on to lose to Sam Snead in the final.

In 1979, in his autobiography, Jack Kramer, a tennis champion after Vines's time, rated Vines as, at the height of his game, the best tennis player ever; Kramer also wrote of Vines that he was "surely the best athlete ever" in golf and tennis. Vines remains only one or two men, the other being Frank Conner (see Chapter 28), to have played in the US Open at both tennis and golf.

Vines died in 1994 at the age of 82.

159. Carl Voss (1907-1993), *American ice hockey player and footballer*

Carl Voss was born in Massachusetts in 1907 but moved with his family to Canada as a teenager.

Voss's first major ice hockey team was the Toronto Maple Leafs, for whom he played in the 1926/27 season; in 1932, he joined the Detroit Cowboys and over the next five seasons played for the Ottawa Senators, the St Louis

Eagles, the New York Americans and the Montreal Maroons before joining the Chicago Black Hawks in 1937. In his first season with the Chicago Black Hawks, Voss won the Stanley Cup, scoring the winning goal in Game 4 against the Toronto Maple Leafs.

Before becoming a professional ice hockey player, Voss played Canadian football (as American football is known in Canada) and represented his university team, Queen's, for four years; in 1924, his first year in the team, Queen's University won the Grey Cup, a cup competition between Canada's leading Canadian football teams. When Voss added the Stanley Cup 13 years later, he became only the second, and last, man to have won both Cups, the other one being Lionel Conacher (see Chapter 27).

Injury put an end to Voss's ice hockey career in 1938, after having played 261 games in the National Hockey League; after retiring as a player, Voss continued to be involved in the world of ice hockey, eventually becoming the referee-in-chief for the National Hockey League, a position he held for 15 years.

Voss died in 1993 at the age of 86.

160. Micky Walford (1915-2002), *English hockey player, cricketer and rugby player*

Micky Walford was born in Norton-on-Tees in 1915.

Whilst at Rugby School, he played for the Public Schools cricket side as well as, for two years, in the England schoolboys' rugby team. After leaving school, Walford went up to Oxford University and, whilst there, he continued with his cricket and rugby, playing in two cricket Varsity matches against Cambridge and three at rugby but, despite being good enough to play in England trial matches at rugby in 1935 and 1937, hockey was his main winter sport; he won a blue in this as well, playing in three hockey Varsity matches.

After graduating, Walford took up a teaching post at Sherborne College, a position he held for 40 years. His teaching allowed him time to continue with his cricket during the school holidays and hockey. He played cricket for Somerset between 1946 and 1953, heading their batting averages in 1947, 1949 and 1950; after 1953, Walford played Minor Counties cricket for Dorset. By the time he finished playing for Somerset, Walford had played 97 games of first-class cricket, scoring 5,327 runs at an average of 33.71, with nine centuries and a top score of 264; his bowling was rarely used but it did bring him eight wickets, six of them in one innings.

Walford played hockey for England 17 times, often captaining the team; in one of his internationals for England, he was joined in the team by his brother David. In 1948, he played at half-back for the Great Britain team at the Olympics in all five of their matches and won a silver medal, with Great Britain losing to India in the final. Two days after the final, Walford was turning out for Somerset at cricket in their County Championship match against Essex.

Walford died in 2002 at the age of 86.

161. Alan Walker (1925-2005), *Australian cricketer and rugby player*

Alan Walker was born in Manly, Sydney in 1925.

Walker played centre at rugby and picked up five caps for Australia between 1947 and 1950. His first Test was against New Zealand, which Australia lost 5-13; a year later, he toured England and France with the Wallabies; in the game against England, Walker scored a try from 70 yards out as Australia won 11-0 but the game against the French was lost 6-13; during the tour, Walker was the top try scorer for Australia with 19 tries.

In 1950, Walker was again picked for Australia, against the touring British and Irish Lions, playing in two of the Tests, both of which the Lions won.

After this Test series, Walker decided to concentrate on his cricket; he had already made his debut for New South Wales in 1948 with his left-arm fast medium bowling and played for them for five seasons; at the end of his first season, he headed the first-class bowling averages with 38 wickets at 13.34. Walker was selected as a member of the touring party for the Test series against South Africa in 1949/50 and, although he took 25 wickets on the tour in 15 games at an average of 20.24, he was unable to break into the Test team, with Ray Lindwall and Keith Miller in the team.

In 1956, Walker joined Nottinghamshire for whom he achieved the rare feat of taking four wickets in four consecutive balls, having taken the last wicket in Leicestershire's first innings and the first three wickets with the first three balls of the second innings. He started the 1957 season by taking seven wickets for 56 against Middlesex at Lord's before going down with mumps but, in 1958, his performances were hampered by an injury sustained whilst playing rugby league for Leigh.

During a cricket career spanning 11 years from 1948, Walker played in 94 games of first-class cricket, scoring 1,603 runs at an average of 17.42 with a highest score of 73 and taking 221 wickets at an average of 27.47, with his best figures being the seven for 56 against Middlesex in 1957.

Walker died in 2005 at the age of 79.

162. Allan Watkins (1922-2011), *Welsh cricketer, footballer and rugby player*

Albert John Watkins, but known as Allan Watkins, was born in Usk, Monmouthshire in 1922.

Watkins played his first game of cricket for Glamorgan as a 17-year-old, just months before the Second World War broke out. During the War, Watkins served as a firefighter and, although it prevented him from playing cricket for Glamorgan, it did not prevent him playing football for Plymouth Argyle and rugby for Pontypool.

After the War, Watkins played four games for Plymouth Argyle in the 1946/47 season before joining Cardiff City but his football career was cut short because of cartilage problems. Watkins also resumed his cricketing career with Glamorgan, making his maiden century for them against Surrey, on a day Plymouth Argyle released him from training.

Watkins' first Test match was when he was selected to play for England in the final Test against the touring Australians in 1948, making Watkins the first Glamorgan cricketer to play in an Ashes Test; fielding at silly mid-off, Watkins was the last cricketer to field a ball hit by Don Bradman as he fielded Bradman's first ball, only for Bradman to be bowled second ball by Eric Hollies – suggestions that Bradman had a tear in his eye, following the warm reception given to him as he came out to bat, were denied by Watkins.

A year later Watkins was in the England team touring South Africa and he became, when scoring 111 in the fourth Test, the first Glamorgan cricketer to score a century in a Test match. Watkins toured with England again in 1951/52, to India, Pakistan and Ceylon (now Sri Lanka). Between 1948 and 1952, Watkins played in a total of 15 Tests; as a left-handed batsman, he scored 810 runs at an average of 40.50, with two centuries to his name and a top score of 137 not out; with his left-arm fast medium bowling, he took 11 wickets at an average of 50.36, with best figures of three for 20.

Watkins continued playing for Glamorgan until 1961; by the end of his career, he had played 484 games of first-class cricket, 407 of them for Glamorgan, in which he scored 20,361 runs at an average of 30.57, with 32 centuries and a highest score of 170 not out and took 833 wickets at an average of 24.48, with best figures of seven for 28. As a close fielder, Watkins was highly enough regarded for John Arlott to comment that "he has caught the uncatchable so often as to make the impossible his normal standard".

After retiring from Glamorgan, Watkins took up the post as cricket coach at Oundle School, a position he held for many years.

Watkins died in 2011 at the age of 89.

163. Willie Watson (1920-2004), *English footballer and cricketer*

Willie Watson was born in Bolton upon Dearne, Yorkshire in 1920.

Watson first played cricket for Yorkshire in 1939 but the Second World War meant that he missed out playing cricket again until the 1946 season. Watson continued to play for Yorkshire until he moved to Leicestershire as captain in 1958, where he stayed until he played his last game, in 1964.

He was first picked to play for England in 1951 and, over the next eight years, played for them in 23 Tests. As a left-hand batsman, he scored 879 runs in his 23 Tests, at an average of 25.85, including two centuries and a highest score of 116; in total, Watson played 468 games of first-class cricket, scoring 25,670 runs at an average of 39.86, with 55 centuries and a top score of 257.

Watson also played as a wing-half at football and, after starting his football career with Huddersfield Town, joined Sunderland in 1946. Watson spent seven years at Sunderland, during which time he was called up to play for England. His first cap was awarded in the game against Northern Ireland in 1949, a fixture which doubled up as a Home Nations match and a qualifier for the 1950 World Cup and a match which England won 9-2. Watson's second match was a friendly against Italy, which England won 2-0. Although Watson was included in the England squad for the 1950 World Cup in Brazil, he did not play in any of their games, which, with hindsight, might well have been a blessing in disguise as England suffered perhaps their most humiliating defeat of all time, a 1-0 loss to the USA. Watson played two more times for England after the World Cup, one against Wales in the 1950 Home Nations, which England won 4-2 and the other against Yugoslavia, in a friendly which was drawn 2-2.

By the time Watson left Sunderland to join Halifax Town in 1954, he had played 211 league games for them and 12 in the F. A. Cup, and scored 18 goals for them – one of his F. A. Cup matches was the match against Yeovil Town in 1949 when Yeovil, then a non-league team playing in the Southern Division, produced one of the greatest giant-killing results in the F. A. Cup by beating Sunderland, playing in Division 1 (then the top division of English football), 2-1. Watson played for Halifax for three years before re-joining them in 1964 for another three years, after which he took up the manager's job at Bradford City.

After two years as manager at Bradford, Watson emigrated to South Africa to become the manager of the Wanderers cricket team.

Watson died in 2004 at the age of 84.

164. J. P. R. Williams (1949-   ), *Welsh rugby player and tennis player*

John Peter Rhys ("JPR") Williams was born in Bridgend in 1949.

Williams played full-back at rugby and spent most of his rugby career at club level playing for London Welsh and Bridgend. He played his first international for Wales in 1969 and his last, his 55th international for Wales, in 1981. Whilst playing for Wales, Williams won the Grand Slam three times and the Triple Crown six times and, in his 55 internationals, Wales won 37 of them, drew four and lost 14 – he scored six tries for Wales and kicked two conversions and three penalties and his record against England was 10 wins out of 10.

Williams was also picked for the Lions teams touring New Zealand in 1971 and South Africa in 1974 and played in all of the Lions' Tests on these tours; on both tours the Lions were victorious, beating the All Blacks 2-1 with one match drawn in 1971 and the Springboks 3-0 with one match drawn in 1974; Williams only scored three points for the Lions but his long range drop goal in the fourth Test of the 1971 tour helped the Lions secure a draw in that Test and, with it, a series win. Williams made himself unavailable to tour a third time with the Lions in 1977, to concentrate on his medical studies.

Williams also played for the Barbarians in their famous win over the touring All Blacks in 1973, playing a part in Gareth Edwards' memorable try, rated by many the best try of all time; after three dummies, Phil Bennett passed to Williams in their own 22, before Williams passed to John Pullin as the ball made its way eventually to Edwards and the All Blacks' try line.

Williams was also a champion tennis player as a junior. In 1966, he won the British Junior Hard Court Championships at Wimbledon, beating the future British Davis Cup player David Lloyd in the final.

Two years later, Williams played at the British Hard Court Championships in Bournemouth, the first tournament of the "Open Era", when professionals were allowed to enter tournaments alongside amateurs. Williams won his qualifying round but lost in the first round to the Australian Bob Howe; after his loss to Howe, Williams arrived in time to turn out as full-back for Bridgend that evening.

Williams qualified as a physician in 1973 and became a Fellow of the Royal College of Surgeons in 1980; in 1977, he was awarded the MBE for services to rugby.

165. Sonny Bill Williams (1985-   ), *New Zealand rugby player and boxer*

Sonny William Williams, better known as Sonny Bill Williams, was born in Auckland in 1985.

Williams played 73 games of rugby league for the Canterbury Bulldogs over four seasons from 2004 before switching codes and playing rugby union for Toulon, for whom he played for three seasons. From 2011, Williams played rugby union for a number of clubs before switching codes again, playing rugby league for the Sydney Roosters.

Williams has represented New Zealand at both rugby league and rugby union. At league he has played for New Zealand 12 times, playing as lock, second row and centre and scored five tries whereas at union, up to the Southern Hemisphere's Rugby Championships in July and August

2015, he has played in 24 Tests for New Zealand playing at centre and on the wing, 16 in the starting line-up and eight coming on as a substitute; to date, he has scored eight international tries at rugby union for the All Blacks and one of his appearances as a substitute was in the World Cup final in 2011 when New Zealand beat France 8-7.

Williams also boxed professionally from 2009 until 2013. By the time he stopped boxing in October 2013 to concentrate on his rugby, Williams had had six professional fights, winning them all and becoming the New Zealand Professional Boxing Association's Heavyweight Champion and the World Boxing Association's International Heavyweight Champion. By stopping boxing in 2013, Williams forfeited his two boxing titles but, 15 months later, he was back in the ring, fighting the American, Chauncey Weaver; Williams maintained his 100% record with a unanimous points verdict in his favour over Weaver.

166. Charles Plumpton Wilson (1859-1938), *English footballer and rugby player*

Charles Plumpton Wilson was born in Roydon, Norfolk in 1859.

After attending Uppingham School and Marlborough College, Wilson went up to Cambridge University, where he won his blue at rugby in 1877, 1878, 1879 and 1880, captaining the team in 1880 and at cricket in 1880 and 1881. He also represented Cambridge in the 25 mile cycle race against Oxford in 1876.

A year after leaving university, Wilson was picked to play rugby for England against Wales, a match in which England scored 13 tries, of which seven were converted and a drop goal; based on the current scoring system England would have won the match 82-0 but, based on the scoring system which applied back in 1881, England won the match 8-0, with one point for each converted try and one for the drop goal.

After graduating, Wilson took up a teaching post at Elstree School, which allowed him to play football for Hendon Town. Success with Hendon

Town in the F. A. Cup and with the Corinthian amateur club earned him international recognition, resulting in him playing in England's fixtures against Scotland and Wales in the first Home International Championships in the 1883/84 season; England lost the game against Scotland 1-0 but beat Wales 4-0.

Wilson also kept up his cricket after graduating and played for Norfolk for four seasons, having also played for Lincolnshire in his last year at university.

Wilson's brother Geoffrey also played football for England.

Wilson died in 1938 at the age of 78.

167. Jeff Wilson (1973-), *New Zealand rugby player and cricketer*

Jeff Wilson was born in Invercargill, New Zealand in 1973.

After leaving school having won secondary schools national titles in field and track events and having played rugby for the national secondary schools rugby team, Wilson had one season with Southlands Rugby Club before joining Otago. He toured with the All Blacks on their tour to Britain in 1993 and, in his first Test match against Scotland, scored three tries. By the time Wilson retired from rugby in 2002 at the age of 28, he had played 71 times for New Zealand, 60 of which were Tests. Playing on the wing or at full-back, he scored 234 points in his Tests, made up of 44 tries (an All Black record until overtaken by Christian Cullen in 2002), one conversion, three penalties and one drop goal. He played in the 1995 Rugby World Cup (in which New Zealand lost in the final to South Africa in extra time) and again in the 1999 Rugby World Cup and, of his 60 Tests, 45 were won, four drawn and 14 lost.

Wilson also played cricket for Otago and was picked as an all-rounder in the One Day International series against Australia in the 1992/93 season. The arrival of the Super 12 Rugby Competition, in which Wilson played for Highlanders, put an end to his cricket until he retired from rugby and, in 2005, Wilson was again selected to play for New Zealand; he made two more appearances but was unable to play to the standard he had played to earlier in his career. In total, Wilson played in six ODIs, scoring 103 runs at an average of 20.60 with a top score of 44 not out and took four wickets at 65 apiece; in his 39 first-class matches, Wilson scored 1,245 runs at an average of 21.84 with a top score of 78 and, with his fast-medium pace bowling, took 129 wickets at an average of 24.13, with best bowling figures of five for 34.

Although he never played Test cricket, Wilson remains the most recent man to have played rugby for one of the 12 countries who are IRB Executive Council Members and cricket for one of the 10 Test-playing countries. Since retiring from playing sport, as well as breeding cattle, Wilson has taken on the role of commentator for Sky Sports and been director of rugby for Otago, as well as a rugby coach.

Wilson's wife, Adine, is a former captain of New Zealand's netball team.

168. Sammy Woods (1867-1931), *Australian and English cricketer and rugby player*

Samuel Moses James Woods was born in Sydney, Australia in 1867.

Woods finished his schooling in England at Brighton College; whilst at Brighton College, he played football in goal for them and for Sussex as well as taking 14 wickets for 27 runs in a cricket match against Lancing College.

After leaving school, Woods played cricket for Somerset before they had been granted first-class status, before going up to Cambridge University in 1888, the same year he was asked to join the Australian cricket team touring England; he played in the three Test matches between England and Australia that year, scoring 32 runs at an average of 8.33 with a top score of 18 and taking five wickets at an average of 24.20 with best bowling figures of two for 35.

Woods played in four cricket Varsity matches for Cambridge, before re-joining Somerset in 1891, by which time they had been granted first-class status and were playing in the County Championship. Woods took over the captaincy of Somerset in 1894, a position he held until 1906 and continued playing for them until 1910. In 1895, he was called up by England for their tour of South Africa and played in all three Tests, scoring 122 runs at an average of 30.50 with a highest score of 53 and taking five wickets at an average of 25.80, with best figures of three for 28.

By the time he retired in 1910, Woods had played in six Test matches, three for Australia and three for England and in 401 games of first-class cricket, scoring 15,345 runs at an average of 23.42, with 19 centuries and a highest score of 215 and taking 1,040 wickets at an average of 20.82, with best figures of 10 for 69. In 1891, he had been Somerset's leading wicket-taker and in 1897 and 1899, was their leading run-scorer.

Woods also played rugby at Cambridge, playing in three Varsity matches. He played both as a back and as a forward. He was first picked for England in 1890 and played in all three of their Home Nations fixtures. In 1891, he again played in all three of their Home Nations fixtures but, in each of 1892 and 1893, played in only two of the fixtures, before missing the 1894 fixtures through injury. In 1895, he again played in all three fixtures. In the 13 rugby internationals Woods played in, he captained England in five of them, including in all the Home Nations fixtures in 1895 and his overall record for England was nine wins and four defeats.

As well as playing cricket for Somerset, Woods also played hockey for them. After retiring as a cricketer, Woods spent the rest of his life in Somerset, where he was immensely popular and well known; he died in Taunton in 1931 at the age of 64.

169. Max Woosnam (1892-1965), *English footballer and tennis player*

Max Woosnam was born in Liverpool in 1892.

Whilst at Winchester College, he played cricket for the Public Schools XI against the MCC at Lord's and, coming in to bat in the first innings with the schoolboys at 65 for 5, he scored 144. After leaving school, he went up to Cambridge University and won a full blue in football, tennis and golf, in which he had a scratch handicap and a half blue in real tennis; he also played cricket for the university side but never played against Oxford to earn a blue in this as well, although he was 12th man for the 1912 Varsity Match. Whilst at Cambridge, he also played football for Corinthians and, on three occasions, for Chelsea.

After the First World War, in which he served on the Western Front alongside the war poet Siegfried Sassoon and in the Gallipoli Campaign, he continued playing football for Corinthians until 1919, when he joined Manchester City. Between 1920 and 1925, Woosnam played 96 games for Manchester City and despite being an amateur, was asked in 1922, at the request of his professional teammates, if he would accept the captaincy, which he duly accepted.

Woosnam's success whilst at Manchester City saw him selected to captain first the English amateur football team and subsequently England's full international team. Woosnam was also invited to captain the British football team playing in the 1920 Olympics but he turned this down as he had already committed himself to representing Britain at the Games in tennis. Woosnam captained the full England team against Wales in 1922 in a match which England won 1-0. Within months after his first full international cap, Woosnam's robust style of play as a defender resulted in him breaking his leg and he was never chosen again to play for the full international team. Woosnam played his last game of football for Manchester City in 1925 and, although he played a few games for Northwich Victoria, stopped playing football in early 1926, due to injuries and business commitments.

During the summer months, Woosnam kept up his tennis and first competed at Wimbledon in 1919. A year later, at the 1920 Olympics in Antwerp, he won the gold medal in the men's doubles with Noel Turnbull and the silver medal in the mixed doubles with Kitty McKane (who, as Kitty Godfree, won the Wimbledon Women's Singles title twice). A year later, Woosnam represented Great Britain in the Davis Cup, captaining the team as well; Woosnam made his last appearance for Great Britain in the Davis Cup in 1924.

For the Wimbledon Championships in 1921, Woosnam had different partners to those he had played with in the Olympics a year earlier but achieved the same success as he had in Antwerp, when he won the men's doubles title with Randolph Lycett and was runner-up in the mixed doubles with Phyllis Howkins. Woosnam's last appearance at Wimbledon was in 1924 when he lost in the second round in four sets to the Frenchman Jean Borotra, who went on to win the singles title that year.

His time away from competitive tennis and football allowed him to spend more time on his snooker and it was not long after he retired from football that he recorded a 147 maximum break at snooker.

In 1934, Manchester City won the F. A. Cup and at the banquet to celebrate their success, Woosnam was introduced by the team's captain as the greatest ever centre-half and captain Manchester City had ever had.

Later in life, Woosnam became a director at ICI but, having been a heavy smoker for much of his adult life, Woosnam died in 1965 at the age of 72 from respiratory failure.

170. Lev Yashin (1929-1990), *Russian footballer and ice hockey player*

Lev Yashin was born in Moscow in 1929.

Yashin first played in goal for Dynamo Moscow in 1950 and four years later was picked for the national Soviet Union team. He was a member of the football team which won the Olympics in 1956 and two years later appeared in his first World Cup. Yashin played in two more World Cups, the 1962 World Cup in Chile and the 1966 World Cup in England and, although he was included in the Soviet Union's squad for the 1970 World Cup in Mexico, did not play in any of their games at that World Cup.

With Dynamo Moscow, Yashin won the Russian league title five times and the Soviet cup three times; with the national team, as well as winning the Olympic gold in 1956, he won the European Championships in 1960 and came fourth in the 1966 World Cup.

Yashin has been given credit for changing the way goalkeepers played; instead of staying on his goal line, waiting to be called into action, Yashin would come off his line to catch crosses and intercept forward passes, something now commonplace amongst goalkeepers but rare in his playing days.

Over his football career, Yashin received numerous awards, including in 1963 the European Footballer of the Year and the Ballon d'Or, the only goalkeeper to have received either of these awards.

Yashin retired from football in 1970, having played 812 games, of which 326 were for Dynamo Moscow and 78 for the Soviet Union; in his 812 games, he saved 151 penalties and kept over 270 clean sheets. After retiring, he continued to receive accolades including being chosen in 1994 by FIFA in their World Cup All-Time Team and again by them in 2002 in their World Cup Dream Team; FIFA also recognised Yashin as the World Goalkeeper of the 20th Century.

As well as playing football for Dynamo Moscow, Yashin also played ice hockey for them and was a member of the team which was the Soviet Cup champions in 1953.

After his playing days were over, Yashin worked for Dynamo Moscow in an administrative role. He died from stomach cancer in 1990 at the age of 60.

171. Sheila Young (1950-), *American skater and cyclist*

Sheila Young was born in Birmingham, Michigan in 1950.

Young competed in the 1972 Winter Olympics in the speed skating events but she won her first medal, a bronze, for cycling at the World

Championships in 1972, in the sprint event. A year later, she won the gold medal at the cycling World Championships and at the speed skating World Championships, a feat she repeated in 1976 when she won her second gold at cycling and her third gold medal in speed skating, having won her second gold in speed skating in 1975.

1976 also saw Young competing at the Winter Olympics and, in the speed skating events in which she took part, she won the gold medal in the 500 metre event, silver in the 1,500 metre event and bronze in the 1,000 metre event.

Young then retired from speed skating but took up cycling again in 1981. In her first year back cycling Young won her third gold medal at the World Championships; a year later, she added a silver to her collection which by then consisted of three golds and one bronze which she had won in cycling events at the World Championships, three golds and two bronzes which she had won in speed skating events at the World Championships and one gold, one silver and one bronze she had won in speed skating events at the Winter Olympics.

Young is now a physical education teacher; her brother Roger competed as a cyclist at the 1972 Olympic Games as did her husband Jim Ochowicz (who also competed at the 1976 Olympics) and their daughter Elli has competed in three Winter Olympic Games in the speed skating events.

172. Babe Zaharias (1911-1956), *American athlete and golfer*

Mildred Ella Zaharias (nee Didrikson and best known as Babe Zaharias) was born in Port Arthur, Texas in 1911, not long after her parents had emigrated from Norway.

After leaving school, Zaharias played basketball for the Golden Cyclones, which won the Amateur Athletic Union's Basketball Championships in 1931.

A year later she was competing in the 1932 Olympics, at which she won the gold medal in both the 80 metre hurdles event and the javelin and the silver medal in the high jump. She also competed that year in the Amateur Athletic Union's Championships, taking part in eight of the ten events; of the eight she took part in, she won five of them and tied for first place in a sixth and, in the space of one afternoon, set new world records in the javelin, the 80 metre hurdles, the high jump and the baseball throw.

By 1935, Zaharias had decided to take up golf. She won her first major in 1940, the Women's Western Open, a title she went on to win again in 1944, 1945 and 1950; in 1946, she won the US Women's Amateur Championships and a year later became the first American to win the British Ladies' Amateur Championships. 1947 also saw her win another of the Women's major golf tournaments, the Titleholders' Championships, a title she won again in 1950 and 1952. Zaharias won the third major which women competed for, the US Women's Open, in 1948 and again in 1950 and 1954. Although three other female golfers, Mickey Wright in 1961, Pat Bradley in 1986 and Inbee Park in 2013, have more recently won three of the majors in the same year, they have done so when there have been more than three majors for the women to compete in; by winning all three majors in 1950, Zaharias remains the only woman to have won the grand slam when there were at least three majors in the year. Zaharias only played one more year after winning her tenth and last major in 1954; Sweden's Annika Sorenstam has matched Zaharias's record of ten majors and only fellow Americans, Louise Suggs with 11 majors, Mickey Wright with 13 majors and Patty Berg with 15 majors have won more.

In 1953, Zaharias was diagnosed with colon cancer and, after a recurrence in 1955, died a year later at the age of 45. At the start of the 21st century, her performances as an athlete and as a golfer led ESPN to name her as the 10th greatest North American athlete of the 20th century, placing her ahead of every other female athlete.

Author's note: In 1974, Sandra Haynie also won the grand slam but there were only two women's golf majors that year.

Appendix 1

Others who played cricket for England and football for an English league club

Cricket Test matches Football club

David Bairstow (1951-1998)	4	Bradford City
Jack Durston (1893-1965)	1	Brentford
Laurie Fishlock (1907-1986)	4	Aldershot, Crystal Palace, Gillingham, Millwall, Southampton
Henry Howell (1890-1932)	5	Wolves, Accrington Stanley, Southampton, Port Vale
Walter Keeton (1905-1980)	2	Nottingham Forest, Sunderland
Phil Mead (1887-1958)	17	Southampton
Cyril Poole (1921-1996)	3	Mansfield
Mordecai Sherwin (1851-1910)	3	Notts County
David Smith (1934-2003)	5	Bristol City, Millwall
William Storer (1867-1912)	6	Derby County
Frank Sugg (1862-1933)	2	Burnley, Derby County, Sheffield Wednesday, Everton
Ken Taylor (1935-)	3	Bradford Park Avenue, Huddersfield Town

Appendix 2

Others who played football for England and first class cricket

Number of football caps Cricket club

C.W. Alcock (1842-1907)	5	MCC
Morton Betts (1901-1942)	1	Middlesex, Kent
Francis Birley (1847-1914)	2	Lancashire, Surrey
George Brann (1865-1954)	3	Sussex
John Brockbank (1848-1954)	1	Cambridge University
Cuthbert Burnup (1875-1960)	1	Kent
Lindsay Bury (1857-1935)	2	Cambridge University, Hampshire
Raich Carter (1913-1994)	13	Derbyshire
Charles Chenery (1850-1928)	3	Surrey
Tommy Cook (1901-1950)	1	Sussex
Norman Cooper (1870-1920)	1	Cambridge University
George Cotterill (1868-1950)	4	Cambridge University, Sussex
Arthur Cursham (1853-18845)	6	Derbyshire, Nottinghamshire
Henry Cursham (1859-1941)	8	Nottinghamshire
Harry Daft (1866-1945)	5	Nottinghamshire
John Devey (1866-1940)	2	Warwickshire
Percy de Paravicini (1862-1921)	3	Middlesex
John Dixon (1861-1931)	1	Nottinghamshire

Graham Doggart (1897-1963)	1	Cambridge University, Middlesex
Willy Foulke (1874-1916)	1	Derbyshire
Billy George (1874-1933)	3	Warwickshire
John Goodall (1863-1942)	14	Derbyshire
R. Cunliffe Gosling (1868-1922)	5	Cambridge University, Essex
Leonard Graham (1901-1962)	2	Essex
Arthur Grimsdell (1894-1963)	6	East of England
Fred Hargreaves (1858-1897)	3	Lancashire
Stanley Harris (1881-1926)	6	Cambridge University, Gloucestershire, Surrey, Sussex
Edward Haygarth (1854-1915)	1	Gloucestershire, Hampshire
Mike Hellawell (1938-)	2	Warwickshire
Arthur Henfrey (1867-1929)	5	Cambridge University
Gordon Hodgson (1904-1951)	3	Lancashire
Anthony Hossack (1867-1925)	2	Cambridge University
Eric Houghton (1910-1996)	7	Warwickshire
Leonard Howell (1848-1895)	1	Surrey
James Iremonger (1876-1956)	3	Nottinghamshire
William Kenyon-Slaney (1847-1908)	1	MCC
Robert Kingsford (1849-1895)	1	Surrey
Arthur Knight (1887-1956)	1	Hampshire
Jack Lee (1920-1995)	1	Leicestershire
Tinsley Lindley (1865-1940)	13	Cambridge University, Nottinghamshire
William Lindsay (1847-1923)	1	Surrey
Lewis Vaughan Lodge (1872-1916)	5	Hampshire
Edward Lyttelton (1855-1942)	1	Cambridge University, Middlesex
Clement Mitchell (1862-1937)	5	Kent
Billy Moon (1868-1943)	7	Middlesex

Ernest Needham (1873-1936)	16	Derbyshire
Cuthbert Ottaway (1850-1878)	2	Oxford University, Kent, Middlesex
Percival Parr (1859-1912)	1	Gentlemen of Kent
George Raikes (1873-1966)	4	Oxford University, Hampshire
Herbert Rawson (1852-1924)	1	Kent
G. O. Smith (1872-1943)	20	Oxford University, Surrey
Harry Storer (1898-1967)	2	Derbyshire
Alfred Stratford (1853-1914)	1	Middlesex
Derek Ufton (1928-)	1	Kent
Fanny Walden (1888-1949)	2	Northamptonshire
Percy Walters (1863-1936)	13	Oxford University
Fred Wheldon (1869-1924)	4	Worcestershire
Herbert Whitfeld (1858-1909)	1	Sussex
S. W. Widdowson (1851-1927)	1	Nottinghamshire
Claude Wilson (1858-1881)	2	Surrey
Jimmy Windridge (1882-1939)	8	Warwickshire
Charles Wreford-Brown (1866-1951)	2	Oxford University, Gloucestershire

Appendix 3

Others who played international rugby and international cricket

1. Argentina

   Carlos Mold (1885-?)

2. Canada

   Cornelius Henry (1956-   )

3. Fiji

   George Cakobau (1912-1989)
   Naitini Tuiyan (1915-2002)
   Nat Uluisiti (1932-2004)

4. Ireland

   Robert Alexander (1910-1943)
   Robert Barnes (1911-1987)
   Harry Corley (1878-1936)
   Michael Dargan (1928-   )
   Arthur Douglas (1902-1937)
   Jim Ganley (1904-1976)
   Lucius Gwynn (1873-1902)
   Arthur Harvey (1878-1966)

Raymond Hunter (1938-   )
Finlay Jackson (1901-1941)
Ham Lambert (1910-2006)
Dickie Lloyd (1891-1950)
Gerry Quinn (1917-1968)
Kevin Quinn (1923-2002)

5.   Scotland

Thomas Anderson (1863-1938)
Alex Angus (1889-1947)
A. G. G. Asher (1861-1930)
Edward Bannerman (1850-1923)
David Bell (1949-   )
John Bruce-Lockhart (1889-1956)
Rab Bruce-Lockhart (1916-1990)
James Carrick (1855-1913)
Thomas Chalmers (1850-1926)
Gerard Crole (1894-1965)
J. N. G. Davidson (1931-   )
Maurice Dickson (1882-1940)
A. R. Don Wauchope (1861-1948)
Alex Duncan (1881-1934)
Thomas Hart (1909-2001)
Frank Hunter (1858-1930)
Andrew Ker (1954-   )
Ross Logan (1909-1993)
Ian Lumsden (1923-   )
Bill Maclagan (1858-1926)
A. S. B. McNeil (1915-1944)
Ken Marshall (1911-1992)
Thomas Marshall (1849-1913)
Stuart Moffat (1977-   )
James Reid Kerr (1883-1963)
Ken Scotland (1936-   )
Henry Stevenson (1867-1945)

James Tennent (1888-1955)
James Walker (1859-1923)

6. Sri Lanka (formerly Ceylon)

Mahesh Rodrigo (1927-2011)

7. Zimbabwe (formerly Rhodesia)

Terence Bowes (1951-   )
Colin Duff (1876-1941)
Craig Evans (1969-   )

8. Two Nations

John Campbell (1877-1917) – Argentina (cricket) and Scotland (rugby)
Gilbert Cook (1911-1979) – Ireland (cricket) and England (rugby)
William Lovat Fraser (1884-1968) – Scotland (cricket) and Great Britain (rugby)
Billy King (1902-1987) – Ireland (cricket) and Singapore (rugby)
James Magee (1877-1949) – Ireland (cricket) and Great Britain (rugby)
Bill Taberer (1872-1938) – Rhodesia (cricket) and South Africa (rugby)

Bibliography

Books

All-Round Genius The Unknown Story of Britain's Greatest Sportsman by Mick Collins

Australian Dictionary of Biography

Benjamin Howard Baker Sportsman Supreme by Bob Phillips

Beyond A Boundary by C. R. L. James

Bounce by Matthew Syed

C B Fry King of Sport by Iain Wilton

City Centre by Simon Halliday

Cloughie Walking on Water My Life by Brian Clough

Cricket: A History of its Growth and Development by Rowland Bowen

David Gower's 50 Greatest Cricketers Of All Time by David Gower

Denis Compton by Norman Giller

Dictionary of Welsh Biography

Dictionary of Ulster Biography

Encyclopaedia Britannica

Higgy by Alastair Hignell

History of University College Oxford by William Carr

JPR: Given The Breaks: My Life in Rugby by JPR Williams

Lottie Dod – Champion of Champions – Story of an Athlete by Jeffrey Pearson

Master Sportsman by Robert Sayer

One Hundred Years of Wimbledon by Lance Tingay

Playing the Moldovans at Tennis by Tony Hawks

Rugby's Greatest Characters by John Griffiths

Sammy: The Sporting Life of S. M. J. Woods by Clifford Jiggens

Seven Years in Tibet by Heinrich Harrer

Shoreline: A Journey Along The South African Coast by Chris Marais and Julienne du Toit

Swanton in Australia with MCC 1946-1975 by E W Swanton

The Autobiography Jackie Stewart Winning Is Not Enough by Jackie Stewart

The Big Train by Richard Brignall

The Concise History of Tennis by Karoly Mazak

The Extraordinary Book of South African Rugby by Wim van der Berg

The Game My 40 Years in Tennis by Jack Kramer

The Golden Age of Cricket by David Frith

The Guinness Book of Records

The Official History of the Olympic Games and the IOC Athens to London 1894 – 2012 by David Miller

The Roses Matches 1919-1939 by Neville Cardus

The Snowy Baker Story by Greg Growden

The Top 100 Cricketers Of All Time by Christopher Martin-Jenkins

The Vic Richardson Story by Victor Richardson

Wisden Cricketers' Almanack 1950, 1953, 1955, 1957, 1962, 1966, 1968, 1969, 1972, 1978, 1984, 1985, 1987, 1988, 1990, 1991, 1994, 1995, 1998, 2000, 2001, 2002, 2004, 2005, 2006, 2008, 2011, 2012, 2013 and 2014

World Cricketers – A Biographical Dictionary by Christopher Martin-Jenkins

1966 And All That My Autobiography by Geoff Hurst

20th Century All-Rounder: Reminiscences and Reflections of Clive van Ryneveld by Clive van Ryneveld

Websites

www.alloutcricket.com

altchetron.com

www.barbarianfc.co.uk

www.blackcaps.co.nz

bluekipper.com

brentfordandchiswicklhr.org.uk

www.cc-publishing.co.uk

cheltcs.councilcricketsocieties.com

www.coloradosports.com

www.cricketcountry.com

CricketArchive.com

www.dailymail.co.uk

www.englandfootballonline.com

espn

www.espncricinfo.com

espn scrum

FIFA.com

www.framcollege.co.uk

greatesthockeylegends.com

www.historytoday.com

hockeynz.co.nz

www.independent.co.uk

www.inute.ac.uk

www.legsidelizzy.com

www.liverpoolharriers.co.uk

www.macla.co.uk

www.mid-day.com

newcastlefans.com

www.northberwick.org.uk

www.oldframlinghamian.com

www.omclub.co.uk

www.opengolf.com

paralympic.org

paralympicanorak.wordpress.com

www.scoop.co.nz

www.scotsman.com

SkateResults.com

spartacu.educational.com

www.sports-reference.com

www.stuff.co.nz

www.teara.govt.nz

www.thecanadianencyclopaedia.ca

James Holder

www.the fa.com
topendsports.com
www.ultimatenzsoccer.com
U.S.SeniorOpen.com
venn.lib.cam.ac.uk
www.where-are-they-now.co.uk
en.wikipedia.org
no.wikipedia.org

Reports

Top 100 Soccer Players Ever by the Association of Football Statisticians

Lightning Source UK Ltd.
Milton Keynes UK
UKOW04n1915051015

259904UK00001B/1/P